ADVANCE PRAISE FOR

You're Not Lost

"Every young woman with a dream should read this book. It's a road map for anyone who feels stuck or doubts their abilities to make their future happen. *You're Not Lost* provides you with the encouragement and step-by-step action plan to help you figure out what you're supposed to be doing and how to make it a reality!"

—ANN SHOKET, author of *The Big Life*
and former editor in chief of *Seventeen*

"*You're Not Lost* is an encouraging and insightful guide to exploring the power of your own inner voice. Maxie invites readers to lean into their own innate wisdom and challenges them to rewrite their narrative about self-confidence. With thoughtful questions and inspired worksheets, this book will help you figure out how to take the next step, even when you're not feeling confident about what's next."

—LATHAM THOMAS, women's wellness maven
and bestselling author of *Own Your Glow*

"I wish I had this book when I was in my twenties, but anyone going through a career transition will benefit from Maxie's tell-it-like-it-is advice too. She reminds us that sometimes you need to start small, avoid getting overwhelmed by outside voices, stop chasing unrealistic goals, and focus on what matters most. It's a modern road map to a happier and more satisfying career path."   —FRAN HAUSER, author of
The Myth of the Nice Girl

"*You're Not Lost* is the pep talk you need when you have no idea what's next. With reminders that you've 'totally got this' to worksheets that help you sort it all out— Maxie gives you all the encouragement you need to feel inspired and ready to take on the world!"   —JACLYN JOHNSON, CEO of Create & Cultivate
and author of *WorkParty*

"Whether you're totally lost about what you should do with your life or just slightly bewildered about next steps, Maxie McCoy's book is packed with inventive and refreshing ideas to energize you and get you on your way."

—KATE WHITE, *New York Times*–bestselling author of
The Gutsy Girl Handbook: Your Manifesto for Success

"THIS book is what I was missing earlier in my career! Dream careers are a wild journey, and the first definitive step to venturing forward on yours is ingesting a dose of Maxie-infused confidence. *You're Not Lost* contains all the kick-self-doubt-to-the-curb tools you need to boldly stride forward to wherever your wildest hopes and unleashed ambitions ultimately lead you."

—KELLY HOEY, author of *Build Your Dream Network*

"Maxie McCoy reminds us that confidence doesn't require control of circumstances, that climbing the ladder doesn't require us to stabilize it too, and that arriving at a worthwhile destination doesn't mean we have planned every detail of the travel itinerary in advance. We can go along for the ride, enjoy the journey, and cross bridges as we come to them, knowing that it's not the luggage we carry—education, credentials—but we, ourselves, who are the difference makers."

—WHITNEY JOHNSON, author of *Disrupt Yourself and Build an A-Team*

"If you're looking for what's next, *You're Not Lost* will help you figure that out. Full of exercises and worksheets, this is a guide for millennial women that will get you thinking about your future and believing in your ability to achieve it."

—TINA WELLS, CEO of Buzz Marketing Group and
author of *Chasing Youth Culture and Getting It Right*

"Everyone feels lost at some point, but not everyone knows what to do about it. Within the pages of *You're Not Lost*, Maxie has given us a clear guide for dealing with those lost feelings. Focused squarely on reminding women of their power and encouraging them into action with memorable interviews, fresh advice, and fun worksheets, this is the perfect guidebook to figuring out what's next for you."

—LAUREN MAILLIAN, author of *The Path Redefined:
Getting to the Top on Your Own Terms*

YOU'RE **NOT** LOST

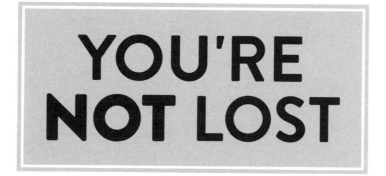

YOU'RE NOT LOST

An **Inspired Action Plan**

for Finding Your Own Way

Maxie McCoy

A TarcherPerigee Book

tarcherperigee
An imprint of Penguin Random House LLC
375 Hudson Street
New York, New York 10014

Most TarcherPerigee books are available at special quantity discounts for bulk
purchase for sales promotions, premiums, fund-raising, and educational needs. Special
books or book excerpts also can be created to fit specific needs. For details, write:
SpecialMarkets@penguinrandomhouse.com.

ISBN 9780143132561

Printed in the United States of America
1   3   5   7   9   10   8   6   4   2

To

The Real McCoys . . .

In a sky full of blessings,
you're my brightest star.

Contents

Primer

You're the one you've been waiting for.
—Byron Katie

It matters how things start.

So, I want you to know this before we begin. There is an escape route from this quicksand of confusion you're feeling, the one that threatens your ability to move forward. Even though it doesn't feel like it, *there is*. Whether it's been months or years of meandering through the dark, I know that the daily search of *Where the hell am I going?* wears even the strongest woman thin. When you're constantly questioning where you're supposed to be and how the hell you're supposed to get there, the quicksand gets even quicker.

One thought multiplies itself like some virus until the bombardment of questions just won't stop:

Is this job the right one?

Did I make the right decision?

Why am I not farther along by now?

Why can't I find something that even halfway fulfills me?
Where should I put down roots and live?
Am I supposed to be doing this for the rest of my life?
Should I be doing something else? Or more?
Am I meant for anything worthwhile?
Will it always feel like this?
Will I ever get there? And where is "there"?
I'm so lost.

With each question and doubt, you struggle a bit more, further distancing yourself from the direction you're desperate for. When this happens, it's easy to lose hope that you'll ever find your way out and get back to knowing (or having some sense of it at least) that you're on the right track.

Wanting just a little bit of clarity about where life is going is *not* too much to ask.

This barrage of doubt often leaves you with *But how did I get here?* How can someone who has worked this hard and piled up a treasure chest of achievements . . . someone who took all the right classes . . . someone who's working hard to create a career (even if it's sucking the soul right out of you) . . . someone who prides themselves on having it all together . . . feel so *not* together?

Because what you're feeling is normal. In fact, I'm not sure I've ever met someone who *hasn't* felt lost at some point. What you must remember in order to pull yourself out of that place of self-doubt sooner rather than later is that *you're not alone.*[1] Which is hard to remember when everyone on Instagram seems like they've got their shit *so* figured out. I know how insanely isolating it feels to believe that you're lost.

Contrary to what you think, feeling lost is actually a wildly wonderful thing. These crap feelings are a part of your process for achieving clarity. Breaking points break you open. They lead you to the light. If you never face these feelings, you'll never have the option to rebuild a path you're fully pumped about.

Breaking points break you open. They lead you to the light.

Let me do some explaining about how you got here (because I have opinions, lots of them). I should probably mention first that you (well, all of us, really) were sold a bill of goods. You were promised that if you followed all the "right" steps, then everything would come together and your future would appear magically with each check on your list of accomplishments. We all believed it, passionately.

But the truth is, we're living in a world that obsesses over achievement and outcomes and misses the messy process of the journey entirely. Maybe you sorta know what you want but you have *no* idea how to get there. Or maybe you're at a total loss for both. Either way, you're handcuffed both to your own obsession with *thinking* your way to a solution and to your belief that dreaming up the "big picture" is going to end the longing for direction in your life.

This obsession with the big picture is everything holding you back (and a fast track to an emotional hell). Life isn't a well-planned trip down Highway 1; you don't need to know where you'll end up in order to begin.

Here's what you *do* need: a deep, deep sense of self-belief. We're talking an ocean of it, swelling to the stars. It's the single most important skill that you're missing in this moment, and the only one that will catapult you into trusting where you're going even if you

You don't need to know where you'll end up in order to begin.

★

can't actually see where it ends. Plus, it'll ensure that you enjoy the process of getting there.

Let me just say that this isn't a blame game. Missing the puzzle piece of confidence, especially as women in this world, is totally normal and understandable. There are so many external messages, cultural constructions, and institutions (ahem, patriarchy, anyone?) that play whack-a-mole with your soul. You're told that if you are not a certain way (race, gender, sexuality, size, status, or fill in the blank) you don't deserve to be here. It grinds you down until you're unsure if you even possess anything worth offering. And it can be hard to push back against it, but we're going to, together, because coming out of your own personal *lost* fog depends on it. *You* get to decide to be confident and to take the actions that will build that confidence. And yes, the brain can be rewired like that.[2]

Confidence in yourself will shine a spotlight on the exit route from your deafening doubt. Conventional wisdom taught you that you need to know where you're going in order to begin, but actually, you'll unlock it all by just beginning. You'll start by starting. You'll take one teeny, tiny step, something small, *today*. And then tomorrow. And the next day. And all the days after it. The steps will get bigger, and you'll feel more and more sure about your path. You'll also be less tolerant of anyone telling you to be different from who you truly are. Your steps won't all be right, but they'll all be forward. Plus, these micro-actions kindle a slow burn of confidence, which will turn into a bonfire of self-believin'.[3]

Small Action ⤖ Confidence ⤖ More Actions ⤖
More Confidence ⤖ Bigger Actions ⤖ DIRECTION

Oh, the bottles of wine I wouldn't have drunk if I'd only known all of this earlier. We often don't associate our feelings of being lost with a lack of self-belief (I didn't), but that's a big part of what's going on. If we did, we'd be out there doing things, trying things, starting things, instead of full-on frozen trying to think our way to the end destination. This is the secret password you've been looking for. And these pages are devoted to helping you create the *right* micro-steps that will build a big, beautiful cycle of self-belief in your life. You'll build it with consistent encouragement to take mini-step after mini-step, each of which is designed to deepen your belief in your abilities and illuminate your direction. We'll say good-bye to the big picture (for now) and hello to the little stuff (immediately).

Let's get a few things straight, though, because hot damn there's so much crap out there about what you should be and try to become. Confidence isn't about being a better or different you. It's about seeing yourself and all that you have and believing in *that*.

Let history remember that I gave you the *actual* definition of confidence, which is **the level in which you believe your actions will have a positive outcome**. This is important because so much of finding your way is trusting that what you do today will lead you somewhere you want to be tomorrow. Your path, the one you're freaking out about, the one you're confused about where it's headed . . . it'll show up when you return to yourself. You'll realize that you've got the skills, and the determination, and the talent to do whatever you want to do. You've got what it takes. It's simply a matter of learning to trust that and trust yourself.

Here's the *really* great news: Like all the other skills you've spent so much time working on, confidence in yourself can be strategized, and it'll get stronger with time and practice.

We're going to leave the big questions about your life in the dust, and instead get crystal clear on the little actions you can implement now. The end result will be the same: You'll eventually shift your mindset from one of lost to one of found, but without having to know exactly how it all ends. You'll realize that you've had the compass in your hand all along. That compass is confidence. It'll get you pushing your dreams forward like you didn't know you could, and throw massive momentum into your everyday interactions. This is so much better than having it all figured out. This is you defining your journey and really enjoying it, like, eating-a-hot-Nutella-crepe-on-the-streets-of-Paris-with-Lady-Eiffel-sparkling-in-the-background enjoying it. Really loving it.

My goal with these pages is to hold up a mirror so you can see what I'd see if we were together catching up in my sunset nook over takeout Thai food: that all of your education and all of your hard work and all of your personal development and all of those unique talents are moving you somewhere you want to be . . . somewhere magical. Even your wrong turns have mattered, because often so much of knowing where you *do* want to go is knowing where you've been and never care to return. We're going to get you the hell out of Dodge.

HOW ALL THIS WORKS

Some of this confidence stuff is an inside job. And even more of it requires you to actually do something—a lot of small somethings, actually. This is going to require some commitment on your end. But it can be done and it pays off big-time. Once you begin to wrap your mind and heart around how much there already is to believe in—how much you *already* are—the doubts that originally held you back will slowly disappear, making way for clarity and action.

I've put together a stiff cocktail of confidence for you throughout this book. I've been where you've been, *big-time*, and most women I know have been here too. Fulfilling life experiences, while still far from perfect, are a very near and very real likelihood for you. I promise, I'd go through the worst of the worst of my days of feeling lost a million times over to get where I am. I would. Because they all led me here. And yours will too.

Let me level-set some of your expectations: I don't know where my life ends up. And neither will you. Unless you happened upon a magic crystal ball, no one does. But trust yourself that through this book you'll be taking the right actions to get to somewhere you want to be—that's the real game changer. I know it in my bones and soon you will too.

The not-so-magical three-word death sentence *I'm so lost* has been uttered in almost every conversation I've ever had with a group of women, no matter what city, state, or even continent. And by the way, we're talking thousands and thousands and thousands of conversations. Because that is what I do—I talk *with* women for a living. Emphasis on the *with*, because I'm not a sociologist, a psychologist, or an -ist of any kind. Other than a feminist. But I am a curious and passionate listener, connector, and storyteller. And that's what these pages were born from—having the unique gift of listening to thousands of young women who felt lost and advising them on their career goals, while listening to experts and leaders who once felt that way too, and connecting the truths in all of our stories to figure out a collective framework for solving this feeling of being *lost*.

No matter how great a cheerleader I am (and I am—I believe *so* much, so utterly much, in every woman and her ability to move forward with blazing certainty), I'll make one thing crystal clear: I can give you the seeds for your garden, but girl, you gotta do the planting. And raking. And resoiling after the thunderstorm. Basically, you gotta do the work. **Because this book isn't the answer. It's here to help you realize that *you* are.** The next pages are about you creating a path forward that is yours and only yours. Always yours. No one, including myself, can tell you how to *find* your path. But I can give you the confidence to create it.

I'll do that by showing you the women who've stood in your shoes, including myself. I'm so excited about the women I'm going to introduce you to. They're confident and inspiring and have figured it out, with a capital *F*. They're living it every day, regardless of not knowing where it'll all lead. Also, I'll be sharing with you what the most recent research is saying about how to make this situation better, and then I'll let you make it about you. Because that's where the shifts happen, when you take all this advice and color it with the trials of your own life to get into action.

SEEK AND YOU SHALL FIND . . .

While you won't find a prescriptive answer to your life in this book, you will find **You've Got This** mini-actions throughout the chapters, meant to be small hits of confidence right to your bloodstream so that you get a feel for what we're trying to implement. And importantly, you'll find **worksheets** at the end of every chapter. They're more in depth and more provocative—not homework, but discovery, and who doesn't love knowing more about themselves? The best way to do these worksheets is to settle into them. Put on some cozy socks, make yourself some tea, and give yourself the space and quiet to let your truth come up. There's no need to rush.

The worksheets conclude with a bigger action, **Do It Now,** which may make you nervous because you *don't* want to do it. But that's why you've gotta. Don't resist—make like a bad Nike ad and just do it . . . *now.*

Just as there are three types of activities, there are also three sections—Ditch, Create, and Rise—and it's not just because three was my favorite number growing up. **Ditch** is where you're going to drop the trapped mindsets that keep you feeling lost. **Create** is where you'll start picking up real momentum by beginning the future you're searching for. And **Rise** will be everything you need to keep going, to keep ascending.

All of this is necessary because tiny micro-actions will eventually lead you to your big picture, to the top of the hill. They'll open up the gates of trust—in yourself. You'll finally see that you don't have to have it all figured out to know you're going the right way.

HOT WITH INTENTION

While I have you, I should let you know about my real intention with this book (because Queen Oprah taught me early on that you don't do anything in life without an intention, and I don't do anything without Oprah). Think about it—the laws of physics (and I'm a big ol' wannabe physics nerd) prove how important intention is through Newton's third law of motion: **For every action, there is an equal and opposite reaction.**[4] So everything you think, everything you do, all the energetic force you put out into the world . . . it's coming back to you. Have more control over what comes your way by being intentional with what you give out.

So here's my intention: This book is written for you from the core of my being, *but* (and don't take this personally) it's not all about you. It's about something bigger, something massive, which cannot be done without you.

When we all tap into an unrelenting belief in ourselves, there's no stopping us. Individually being here, using our voices, showing up, knowing what we stand for, and pursuing the life that sets our soul on fire will inspire others to do the same. Reckoning with our own authentic power at scale will lead to the global rise of women. And that's why I'm here; that's my intention for writing this, for speaking to you: *so that we may rise.*

Because when we have more women in positions of leadership, we'll have more women fighting for the prosperity of others, we'll create more jobs and new ways of doing things that are desperately needed, both here and in developing countries, we'll speak up against injustice, and ultimately, we'll create a world that works toward the well-being of all. And that's a world that's better for every last one of us. We all need some heroes right now, and confidently showing up in our lives allows us all to create solutions and incite change. We are those heroes.

Confidence is fundamental to our collective future. Give yourself this gift so you can start to pay it forward. It all starts with you.

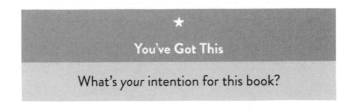

★

You've Got This

What's *your* intention for this book?

1
Ditch

CHAPTER 1

99 Problems
but *You* Are Not One

Don't compromise yourself.
You are all you've got.
—JANIS JOPLIN

L OST IS A *FEELING*. It is not who you are. It does not define you. It's not your identity. And it's sure as hell not a reflection of your worth as a human. Is it a problem? Sure. But you are not your problems.

The sooner you peel away all the layers of what you think you need to change before you're ready to follow your gut, the sooner you'll step into an unobstructed awareness of where you're supposed to be. Peel and shed. Peel and shed. Your path forward will become clearer as you explore and unapologetically accept who you are at your core (*according to you and only you*). This return to yourself is so deeply tied to where you're headed.

A few years ago, a young woman asked me what my single best piece of career advice is. *Only one?* Yes, she said. *And only my best?* Yes, she said again.

At first I gave her a wide-eyed look that said, *I don't think I can distill it all down to just one.* And then as quickly as I wanted to give up on making a single choice, the answer pushed its way forth from the deepest chambers of my heart.

Ahhhhh, I know it, I said. Because I felt it.

"Work every damn day to be the highest possible expression of yourself," I told her. Because when you do, you'll attract all the right people and opportunities to your path in ways that didn't previously seem possible. Being exactly who you are is a powerful energy force. It's a sincerity that people can feel and see, and it opens up the doors to the next step more quickly.

> **Work every damn day to be the highest possible expression of yourself.**

So much of continuing to forge the right path and find the direction that feels so core and true to you is acknowledging the truth of who you are and not letting *anyone* squash it. No matter how much that expression fits into what other people think you should be or do. You are not to blame for being lost. And you are most definitely not at fault for your feelings of *less than* because you haven't found your way (yet). There are no fingers to point here. There's only celebration for who you are, as you are.

What do I mean by the "highest possible expression of yourself"? Everything. The way you express yourself is literally everything, from the hobbies you enjoy, the skills you're interested in, and the opinions you have to the hair you keep and the emotions you feel. It's honoring and loving and, most important, *expressing* what you really feel, are, and desire.

If you want to dye your hair purple and shave half of it off, do it. If you want to begin a company that no one understands, do it. If you've got thoughts on the future of the world that no one agrees with, say 'em and create them. If people think you're too this or too that, eff 'em. Holding onto all those things that flare you up and feel so right is you asking to be recognized from within.

The highest expression of yourself is doing *what* you want to do *how* you want to do it—and being as wildly you as possible while you do.

Seven-year-old me dancing naked in front of my floor-to-ceiling bay windows on the second story for all my little neighbor friends to see (because I was clearly feeling myself and just didn't give a damn) is the wildly expressed self I'm always trying to come back to. Not because I'm a now-closeted exhibitionist, but because the essence of that little girl was one that was so highly expressed and unashamed about it.

That person is there in all of us. She hasn't gone away. The young, wildly expressed woman is in there; you just have to let her take the reins. She's your key to feeling amazing in your skin. She's key to feeling unapologetic about your choices. To using your voice in the big moments and the little ones. She's key to pursuing the next step even when you're worried and unsure, and to continuing to do that in the face of doubt, criticism, and uncertainty. You'll see that you never were the problem. And the sooner you believe that (by identifying all the negative sources and cultural messages that led you there), the easier it'll be to move forward.

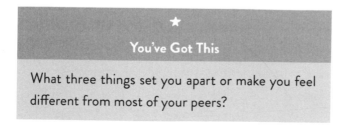

★

You've Got This

What three things set you apart or make you feel different from most of your peers?

GIRLS GONE WILD

We can't talk about building self-belief without also talking about all the reasons it can be hard as hell to be who we really are. That young, wildly expressed person living within you *can* be hard to come back to if you're not aware of why you got away from her in the first place. There's no cheerleading confidence without also acknowledging that we live in a society where being a woman is politicized, where we're consciously and unconsciously made to question ourselves so that our power is tempered. It's a well-oiled and methodical machine meant to keep us small.

The patriarchy is a bitch. It's characterized by being "male dominated, male identified, and male centered."[1] And it's a system that we're born into that we're led to believe can't and shouldn't be changed. We're convinced by that very same system and all those who have internalized it that there are no alternatives. It's the same system that not only ushers us into believing that women should remain in subordinate roles in society but also contributes to other forms of oppression, like racism, homophobia, and sizeism.[2]

And as Gloria Steinem says, oppression wouldn't work unless some of it was internalized.[3] So we start to believe that until we look like X, act like Y, and have the success of Z, we have problems that need to be solved first. The only problem that needs to be solved is trying to fit into the patriarchy's mold.

Keep the TV on for two hours and you're given all the messages of the mold someone wants you in—a laundry list of **things you should desire:**

Skin that color
Partner that perfect
Clothes like that
Hair that soft
Friendships that cool
Thighs that smooth
Boobs that perky
Bank accounts that full
Attitude that chill
Lips that plump
A career that crushes it

And all the things you shouldn't be:

In charge
Aggressive
Emotional
Opinionated
High achieving
Manipulative
Loud
Assertive
Breadwinning
Angry

These qualities aren't wrong. The only thing *wrong* is someone or a group of someones making us feel like we need to change in order to begin. And as G. D Anderson wrote, "Feminism isn't about making women strong. Women are already strong. It's about changing the way the world perceives that strength."

Multiply this completely *non*diverse cultural image of success and womanhood by decades and you end up with some seriously good reasons to believe that the highest expression of yourself is one that's not going to be accepted. But **a woman tapped into her deepest power becomes a massive threat to the status quo.** A woman who knows that she doesn't need anything else to forge her path . . . a woman who knows she already has everything she needs . . . a woman who believes in her right to be here . . . when you're tapped into that, your deepest power, there's literally no stopping you.

When I think about women who do this well, women who don't let anything stop them from saying and doing what they want, Maxine Waters, Jennifer Lawrence, and Beyoncé come to mind. They're vocal about what they believe. They are who they are. And they're *different* from most of the people we see and know. They're living proof that you can be fully yourself and still be successful.

★

You've Got This

List five women who are unapologetically themselves. Look to these women anytime you're second-guessing yourself.

The farther you get from embracing yourself, the farther you get from trusting your own path. And it's hard, I know, especially if you're already feeling lost. Because alongside the messages you receive from society saying you're not good enough, there are always going to be people telling you to be someone or something you're not.

I've never felt so far away from my truth than when I was working for someone who monitored what I wore, if my nails were chipped, how much I talked and how loudly, the phrases I used, the people I hung out with, and what I was writing on social media. The onslaught of opinions was a chute of water that, while likely not intentional, was dousing the fire of expression within me. I was gradually turning down the volume of who I was to fit who this person expected me to be. It heightened all of my insecurities about what I was in the world to do, and how to do it. Let's just say that a few months after I ended this job, my sister's first response was, "I'm so glad to have the *real* you back."

When someone is consciously or unconsciously squashing your self-expression—whether that's a partner, family member, boss, friend, or just the goddamn internet—you've got to fight like hell to gain distance from it. Because you need your differences, your true expressed self, as much as the world does.

Collectively, we aren't one version of a person, and holy shit if that's not the greatest gift. Our diversity in what we look like, how we act, what we desire—not to mention the color of our skin, the type of upbringing, our sexuality, our size, our way of life, and our viewpoints—allows others to rise. We know that in business, companies with more gender, racial, and ethnic diversity outperform their competitors who don't share the same levels of inclusivity.[4] It should be intuitive, then, that when we individually embrace our differences, ignite them, and find our personal footing, the same will happen for our lives.

ALL COMPARISON KILLS IS YOU

Sometimes I actually wonder if Instagram was created for the sole purpose of making us all feel like we're totally shit humans. Between the insanely trendy fashion bloggers, the fitness models who finish off dessert with ten-pack abs, and all of our friends' amazing vacations, accomplishments, and parties, it's no wonder we develop additional complexes when it comes to being ourselves and living our own lives—the ones we're missing 'cause we're too busy scrolling.

You know how this goes. You'll be trucking along, doing your thing, making some progress when wham-bam-fuck-you-ma'am, you see something that makes you feel like you're never going to get there, the *there* there. If you're feeling weird about your hair, you'll find the person with amazing flow. If you're feeling shitty about your job, you'll find the person who just won an amazing award doing what you wish you were doing. And so on and so on. You're so focused on everyone else that you don't see everything that *you've* done and everything *you've* created and everything *you are* that's going to get you exactly where *you* are supposed to be.

It really feels like ten steps back, and sometimes it can be, because comparison puts you into such a stalled-out place that you feel paralyzed and defeated and don't even want to act.

Researchers have found that more than a third of people reported being unhappy following their most recent experience on Facebook, and much of that unhappiness was attributed to envy.[5] It's not surprising, and I'd venture to say that most of us can *feel* how much this constant look into other people's highlight reels plays into how we feel about ourselves and the path that we're on.

One place I can guarantee you won't find the answer to *Where am I going?* is in pictures of other people's lives. In their glossy display of their path, their career, their perfectly designed reading corner, something major is missing: the whole story. Logically, your brain *knows* that what you're seeing isn't the whole story, but the anxiety, weirdness, and envy that bubbles up in your chest makes you feel like you don't even have what it takes to get started. If you can't be there, you don't want to be here. You minimize yourself and your abilities because everything you're seeing looks so much better than where you are.

If you want to tap into the brightest you, then **pay attention to how much time you spend paying attention to others.** Finding your direction requires focusing on *your* greatness. Whether it's about social media, your friends, people in magazines, or humans on TV, you've got to pay attention to you. Because doing you gets way harder when you're trying to be them. And you are the only one who will determine the direction your life is going to take. You're the only one who's going to be taking step after step after step to realize your own path. You need yourself.

> Doing you gets way harder when you're trying to be them.

★

You've Got This

1. Scroll: Set a timer for five minutes. Browse through social media until the time is up.
2. Journal: Write for two minutes about everything you're feeling from scrolling.
3. Assess: Are these productive feelings? Because awareness is everything.

GO YOUR OWN WAY

Your truth is your map. And when it comes to not just *being* the most of you but *doing* the most of you, there will be an onslaught of opinions and templates for how you can move up and move onward. Being the highest expression of yourself includes not only who you are but also how you create what onward looks like. You've got to trust your map even if it's not the path you see everyone else taking.

Of course there will always be *a good way of doing things*. But listen here and listen close: If that *way of doing things* doesn't sit right with you, don't do it. We wouldn't have some of our greatest leaders if they weren't willing to be themselves, think for themselves, and create their own way.

We also need to remember that one person's desired outcome doesn't have to be our own. You don't have to want what other people tell you to want. You don't have to desire what everyone else desires right now. You can be on your own timeline for your own path. You have to get clear on what *you* want versus what other people are telling you to want. Separating the two matters.

One person's successful path may be something to learn from, but at the end of the day you have got to make your journey your own. You've got to do it yourself. I always look to Adele as someone who has gone her own way and made such a beautiful, big mark while doing it.

She doesn't look like other superstars. She doesn't act like other superstars. She doesn't talk like them. She doesn't promote her work like them. She isn't in the limelight like them. She doesn't use social like they do. And here she is, one of the bestselling female artists of all time. Because she's radically sincere. So her.

If you've ever seen a racehorse in training or one pulling a carriage, you'll notice that they have little blinders attached to their bridle that prevent them from seeing beside or behind them. This is done so that they don't get distracted or spooked by what's going on around them; it keeps them squarely focused on themselves and their next step forward.

You need your own set of bridle blinders so that you can commit to coming back, and back again, to yourself—to what feels true, to what feels real, to what feels honest, and ultimately to what feels like the highest possible expression of who you are.

So how do you keep your blinders on to avoid comparing?

* Minimize the time you spend looking at other people's lives.
* Focus on your own life and goals.
* Remind yourself that life is about the process, not the outcomes.

* Give. Expose yourself to people and communities with far less than you have.

Be more of you, not less of it.

* Accept yourself exactly how you are and where you're at. Literally say it: "I accept myself exactly as I am."
* And most important, **be more of you, not less of it.**

MOLDS ARE LIMITS

Remember the last time you made sugar cookies, the ones that are creatively shaped into butterflies, flowers, and hearts? I'm no baker, but luckily my big sister is a professional, magical one. Every time I see her busting out one of her many cookie cutters I watch, sadly, as the sugary, gooey, heavenly goodness that is her dough gets trimmed at the edges.

Whether you're salivating or not ('cause damn, her cookies are good), realize the molds that work for making cookies don't work for our lives. Because you can't afford to lose that dough trimmed at the edges. You can't afford to lose an ounce of your own goodness.

Less, less, less, lesss, lesss, lessss. Trying to fit into a mold means you are *desperately* trying to lessen in order to change. And when you lessen, you're putting a very real limit on yourself. It's exactly what molds are: limits. Cold, hard limits. You have to become less of yourself to stay in the limit of a mold. And why in the actual hell would you want to do that to yourself?

When I was trying to get my footing in broadcasting, my first career, I had this mold I saw everywhere for the type of woman who was successful in that industry. She was small (I'm tall). She was thin (I'm all curves). She had really glossy, smooth hair (I've got a head of tight curls that require a mean blow dryer, a big brush, and a hot flat iron if I want to smooth them out). I was *more* than everything that I was seeing. More inches on my hips. More volume in my hair. More space to my stature.

I tried, *really* tried to fit this mold by being less. I became obsessed with feeling like *too much* and couldn't shake the minute-by-minute assault on my thoughts. I was consumed with minimizing myself, although I didn't realize it at the time. I truly, deeply believed these things had to change if I was going be successful in broadcasting. And it ate at my confidence in such a meaningful way that I actually believed it was holding me back from my big sportscaster dream. Underneath everything I did, it was there.

Limits aren't always about looks and image (for me, at that time in my journey, they were). But they are always about being less—less of our true selves. And what I didn't see was that the more I worked to get closer to the *real* me—who she was, what she looked like, what she cared about—the more exactly what I needed would find me.

The easiest way to get lost is by blending in.

How can future ideas, dreams, and plans find you if you're too busy camouflaging yourself? Where do others end and you begin? Be more of you; be more seen.

If you have a running list of things you think need to change in order for you to find your way, you've actually found the perfect formula in reverse. Take that list and *do not* change those things. Take that list and magnify everything on it. Be more. Take up more space.

You don't really have *anything* to lose, because trying to trim yourself, to fit, to mold, hasn't worked, has it? The mold you're trying to shimmy into is actually a suffocating limit, keeping you from everything you want to be.

WHERE YOU ARE, RIGHT NOW

I know the feeling, intimately, of believing that I couldn't start my dreams *until*.

And because of that feeling, I've told myself some crazy shit on the pathway to figuring it out. I've convinced myself I couldn't successfully pitch myself until I had that perfect one-liner and offering. That I couldn't start pumping out new video content until I had the right equipment. But all these things were external manifestations of believing I had problems to solve in order to be "ready."

I needed to talk better. Look different. Have more experience. Know my tagline. I created hurdles to obsess over, ones that I needed to jump in a major way in order to begin—to figure out where I was going, to believe that I deserved the dream teeming inside me.

And this is what we do, collectively. We tell the small seeds of hope and creativity within us that they don't deserve to be seen yet. That we need to change. That we need to get better. That we need to be less of this or more of that. And *then*, then we'll start. Then we'll move. Then we'll step. Then we can.

That *then* will never come. Because there's absolutely nothing that needs to change about you in order to find your way. Not a thing. You simply and brilliantly only need to recognize it, to believe it, and to honor yourself *exactly* as you are.

This radical acceptance will do wonders for your willingness to follow the directions that are already in your hands. You don't have to become smarter to begin. You don't need to be a better writer to begin. You don't need thicker hair to begin. You don't need more successful friends to begin. You don't need to be more aggressive or more eloquent. You don't *need* anything. You just need you. The you who has cast aside the expectations and opinions about who you should be, how you should act, and what you should desire, and instead follows the only real path out of this feeling of confusion: your truth.

★

You've Got This

List everything you believe you need before you can begin something you want. Now consider what it would feel like to let that all go.

BE WHAT OTHERS NEED TO SEE

The problem with carbon-copy humans isn't just that they're completely devoid of originality and not living their truth; it's that they're one less inspiring example of a fiercely, unapologetically unique human being successful. And I don't just mean successful in the ways we currently measure that in our careers; I mean deeper—in joy, fulfillment, honesty, and integrity. Those who choose to be their own kind of unicorn not only give themselves the gift of truthful living, they are an example to others.

When someone sees you being *fully* you, it gives them the encouragement to be fully *them*. When you own who you are, your own individual story, and all the things that make you you while making you different, you open up infinite possibilities for the people witnessing you.

When you don't take someone's shit in a meeting because you refuse to be disrespected for your gender . . . when you don't blend into the crowd . . . when you operate based only on what's important to you . . . when you call things out . . . when you take some heat and don't let it melt you . . . when you go against the grain of what's expected of you . . . you give others permission to do the same.

Ending the cycle of dampening your true expression to fit in is immeasurably important, not just for you but for others. So if you can't do it for yourself, do it for the woman trying to find her own footing in this world. And do it for future you, because you're going to need yourself—your full self—to get moving on figuring this path out. *Fuck fitting in.* It doesn't serve anyone other than those telling you to do so.

WORKSHEET
Beyond the Box

Awareness is how we start. What norms or molds do you find yourself trying to fit into?

If those norms no longer existed, what would you stop or start doing?

Whose opinions or voice do you hear in the back of your mind the most when making decisions or choices?

Is this a supportive or a judgmental voice?

```
┌································································┐
:                                                        :
:                                                        :
:                                                        :
└································································┘
```

Is there any step that you're not taking due to outside voices and opinions?

```
┌································································┐
:                                                        :
:                                                        :
:                                                        :
:                                                        :
:                                                        :
:                                                        :
:                                                        :
└································································┘
```

★ Do It Now

Act on one thing you've held back from because of someone else's opinion of who you should be. Example: *I held a* PUSSY POWER *sign at the Women's March and posted it on all my social channels* despite knowing it'd piss off some people—including a few people I love—who have very different views than I do.

CHAPTER 2

Appreciate the Ascent

Instant gratification will get you stoned, drunk,
or pregnant. Everything else is going to
take some time.

—ASHLEY LONGSHORE

I'M NOT ONE FOR FIGHTING WORDS, but when I felt lost, anytime someone told me, "You're exactly where you're supposed to be," I felt like maybe a fight was exactly what they'd get from me. Because where I was wasn't where *I* thought I was supposed to be. I wanted to be *there*. There, on the side of life I desired, even though I didn't know what it was or how I'd ever get it. I brimmed with resentment that anyone could think it was that easy when I felt so discontent. *Easy for you to say; you're not as lost as me.*

This is probably a terrible time to tell you that what they said is true. When you're feeling lost, you're actually on a glorious pathway of examination. And the process of finding answers is something that you can't always force. They reveal themselves along the way, and on a timeline that is anything but short. Getting to where you want to be is going to take way longer than you expected and way longer than you'd like. You're not behind, you're not off track, and you're not going to feel this way forever. You're simply on your way. And you'll always be on your way. In order to not permanently feel like that's hell, you have to learn to look around instead of constantly looking ahead. Around you is what you're a part of. It's what's happening. It's where your life actually is right now.

We all have this tendency to want to be at the light at the end of the tunnel before we've even entered it, to be at the top of the mountain—where we think everyone else is hanging out. We expect to snap our fingers and be there, basking in the warm sunshine of success. But unfortunately there's no fast way to get there. Instead, there's just a long, uphill walk—one that gets rocks in our shoes and takes seven times longer than Google Maps predicted. But that journey is as much a part of the experience as taking in the views at the top.

Contrary to your instincts—and the feelings that led you to this book in the first place—you're not always supposed to jump out of your discomfort immediately. It's actually perfectly OK to feel like shit about your life, and even to wallow in it. I know most of the messaging around you says otherwise—and you're constantly being told about all the things you can do, buy, and experience to get out of it—but that's not the journey. The real journey, the one that summons clarity and gives you meaningful direction, is fraught with questioning.

When I was in the early stages of venturing beyond my own feelings of *lost*, I was in an unfulfilling state of limbo. I had settled into a valley of fear and indecision about where I was actually going next. On one hand, I had a vision for how work as my most expressed self looked, and on the other hand, I had security. And while I stood still on the median of that indecision, I beat myself up for feeling what I was feeling: scared, unsure, nervous. Simultaneously, I searched for anything that would make me *not* feel these feels. I wanted them gone, like, yesterday.

In an effort to feel better, we distract ourselves. I was the queen of it while I was feeling lost. I said yes to everything, social and work commitments alike. Filling up my time kept me from examining my truth. I convinced myself I was too swamped for hobbies or creativity. And I got on a plane any chance I could, sometimes when necessary and sometimes not. Distraction is disguised as a good intention to feel anything but what we're currently feeling. And when that doesn't work, we end up more frustrated, which leaves us feeling even more off course than before. "Busy" is complete bullshit, and if you distract yourself with it, you miss the personal discovery that occurs during your ascent.

While I was spending one Saturday afternoon with a friend and mystic (so naturally she's always on point with the truth), I explained my checklist of everything I was doing to figure this limbo out. I had a running list of solutions, complaints, and changes I'd need to make before I would feel better about where my life was headed. And she responded with straight love but unbending truth, asking me to consider that I wasn't supposed to "just get out of this." Maybe the only thing I needed to do to move forward was to *sit in my shit*.

Sit in my shit. . . . It felt true and right and relieving. I could feel myself breathe again. It was the first time I had considered the possibility that the right next step wasn't a step at all. The right next step

was to sit my ass down and feel what was going on. To ask myself *why*
I felt the way I did instead of *how* to stop feeling it. When I did that,
when I halted my own seeking and rolled around in the crap, I found
the confidence to do what I needed to do, because I knew what I was
actually feeling. The confusion melted off and left behind a deeply
rooted knowing about what was next. That certitude was all the belief I needed to actually move forward.

Remember, all the uncertainty and discontent you're experiencing
as a result of feeling lost is helpful. It's all data. The negativity you feel
is informing future positives. And the positives are a feedback loop
that will keep you going. Even though I know you'd like the nega-
tives to be positives right this second, don't breeze through them and
miss the lessons they can teach you.

But I know. I knoooow. Patience is the ultimate bitch. So, if this
is one of your finer virtues, I applaud you for being a modern-day
urban legend. Most of us tend to want to arrive at the finish line
without having to run to get there. And I'm *so* guilty. A dose of patience could help all of us, though, because settling into acceptance
that this is all going to take *way* longer than you think might just be
the ultimate enlightenment for your path.

And there's a gaping difference between having patience and being inactive. Being stalled out will keep you feeling lost. Practicing
patience in your journey will affirm that you have direction to begin
with. Delays are real, and the more we can learn to tolerate them in
our hunt for direction, the better off we'll be. But the beauty of this
waiting game is that anything is possible. *Anything.* A whole universe
of possibility awaits, provided you don't rush toward specific outcomes. Being patient in this process means you're given the gift of

choosing where and who you want to become. It's what'll keep you going, putting one foot in front of the other, no matter what.

I know waiting to get to the outcome can feel like purgatory. Especially when you're looking around and so many people seem like they're up on that mountaintop already enjoying the view. But I'd argue if you *really* knew what was going on for them, it might seem like anything but. Where you're at isn't purgatory at all; rather, it's a bridge, the link between now and then, one that gives you a momentary elevated glimpse into what's ahead.

Diving deeper into your problem will bring more clarity than escaping it ever could. Because you get to examine all the hardest hard parts. Look your fear and discomfort in the eye for what they really are and force yourself to face how you really feel. And you'll find that what's staring back at you is the encouragement you need to figure out what is next. Because when you slow down to feel your feelings instead of running to escape them, you allow the things you really care about, the truth of what excites and energizes you, to catch up, to show themselves, to present. The pain of your problems will push you to the eventual solutions.

★

You've Got This

Ask yourself what you're feeling . . . and then ask why . . . and ask why again . . . and then ask why one more time (three times total). With every answer to why, you'll get a deeper understanding of what's really going on in your head.

We've gotta get comfortable with where we're at in order to get where we want to get. The latter takes time, so much time. Whatever you want to do is going to take way longer than you think. It's hard to see that when you can post a picture and immediately get feedback, when you can shoot an email and get a response in minutes, when the internet can give you answers almost as quickly as you have questions. We live in a culture accustomed to instant gratification. Your path, however, isn't remotely wired that way. You can't get to the top of the mountain just by looking at it. You have to *climb*, and find pleasure in the climbing.

Regardless of how lost you feel, you can begin to feel found from exactly where you are—rather than expecting to get there only when you reach the mountaintop. It's a mindset shift. Found is trusting that your path is the right one. Found is knowing you have direction. And you do. All the bad days you're experiencing and all the frustrated emotions you're feeling are a very real and very important step in the process of getting you to where you want to be. What would happen if you stopped wanting to "be there" and instead just stayed here, right here in this moment . . . with where you are today?

DISTRACTIONS DO NOTHING BUT DETRACT

When someone practically runs you over in a parking lot, it doesn't always blossom into a decade-long friendship. Luckily, in my first few weeks interning on ESPN's campus in Bristol, Connecticut, I met the person who would become my first work bestie. Not because our cubes were near each other, but because she almost reversed over me in her little blue Chevy.

During that time, Kristen Gray was both a friend and peer mentor, the budding video production queen who wasn't an intern but a contractor. I, on the other hand, was someone with no idea what I wanted outside of my deep desire to be successful on-air talent. She took me under her generous and enthusiastic wing to help me with my broadcasting reel, driving me to random fields in Connecticut so we could shoot fake segments about a make-believe sports game that we'd made up on the fly.

As we grew up and I watched her from afar, it seemed like she glided beautifully from a career in video production to life as a military wife and new mom, and then on to an amazing design career and printmaking shop on Etsy. What I didn't know was that between those three careers were a lot of confusion and years of feeling lost. And a whole lot of distracting herself from the truth. Which is what most of us do when we first feel lost.

In the same way that we don't want to sit in our shit, we don't want to sit in a space of unknowing. So we distract ourselves in order to ignore it. Anything to hide the fact that not only are we not living our truth, we don't even know what that truth might be. The distractions take on a lot of the same looks—we apply for a new job because *Why not? It's gotta be better than this.* We let the craziness of life take over everything and we refuse to sit still. We do literally anything other than nothing, because nothing would leave space for an awareness that distractions don't.

That's exactly what Kristen told me she did for a time. At one point she had whiteboarded her life and filled a big poster board with everything she hoped for, dreamt of, or felt passionate about. It was a treasure chest of words that meant nothing and everything to her. And then she did what we do when the answers don't come immediately: She shoved it under the bed and told herself not to think about the truth sitting on the page. She didn't want to think about it because she didn't know what to do with it. What did any of it mean? Or rather, how did it translate into something?

Meaning doesn't always come from executing. Sometimes meaning comes simply from knowing that it's there.

For Kristen, doing something about those words on the page didn't happen until her loving husband found the poster and she was forced to face the fact that she'd been shoving the desire for more in her life as far back as that paper. She was the first to admit to me that she threw herself into the distractions of life so she wouldn't have to focus on her own lack of answers. But twenty-four hours after that poster resurfaced (which, let's not sugarcoat it, was full of tears and tough conversations), a little inspiration to do something creative came to her. And there's been no stopping that momentum since. She's living her most creative, expressed life as a designer with a bangin' Etsy store and confidence to continue growing her pursuits instead of stuffing her ideas under the bed.

While so often we want to take our mind off that pull for something *more*, because we have no idea what it is or how to get there, that doesn't really lead us anywhere.[1] Yeah, your distractions might make you forget that longing for more, or help you feel less uncomfortable for a hot second. Distractions won't, however, help you learn to wait; they'll just prolong your hope of finding direction.

BUT YOU ALSO CAN'T FORCE THE FUNK

In the same way you can't make answers appear out of thin air in your life, you can't force your own process of finding direction. You have to trust that this experience you're in is showing you something about yourself, because if you do, the answers will indeed come . . . in their own time.

And my God could we all take a little bit more time with things. You have to honor exactly where you're at in order to free yourself from feeling lost.

THE CASE FOR TAKING YOUR TIME

There's quite the misconception that "trusting the process" means you should do nothing. While the discrepancy seems minor, it's actually night and day. Trusting the process of finding your way doesn't mean that you sit back with a glass of wine and Netflix and let your future find you. Rather, you stop doing the hard hustle of obsessing over your future in your head and trade it in for hard work wrapped in immense trust.

You'll pull the goodness of the future toward you by being seriously present in your own life right now.

Because you're human (surprise!), the balance of those scales often gets tipped. It gets tipped by distraction, by hustling, by doing anything and everything to forget that you don't actually know what it is you want to be doing. It gets tipped anytime you have a sense of where you want to be but want that outcome now, right now.

Striving strangles. The life-giving air of showing up for your life and simply experiencing the experience goes right out the window when you're constantly hustling for more. When you want to reach the peak of the mountain too much, wanting becomes poison and your goals become the quiet administrator of a lethal injection that you don't see coming.

I've seen my knuckles turn white from holding the steering wheel of desire so tight—too damn tight. It's always clear when you're doing it, because it takes over all of your waking thoughts—you constantly think about your thinking, and rethink how to bring everything you want together, how to get where you want to go. Everyday activities like a workout somehow turn themselves into obsession sessions. Lying in bed trying to sleep is like riding a merry-go-round gone loose in your head. Aimlessly scrolling on social becomes an all-out assault, showing you everywhere you haven't yet arrived.

Days become a race to "figure it out," whatever that actually means. But what if you told yourself that it was perfectly OK to take your time? What would happen if "it" didn't have to happen right now, right this moment, even right this year?

I'll tell you what might occur, learned from the hell of personal experience. What happens when you give yourself permission to slow down and not have all the answers is that you actually feel yourself again. You stop obsessing over the uncertainty and ease into the journey of figuring it out. You begin to seek direction instead of destinations. And that's enough to change everything.

I had to learn my own lesson in the difference between appreciating the ascent and obsessing over it, with a little old-school storytelling. I was recounting my experience of wanting to be where I wasn't yet to my friend Nichole over tea. She listened to me explain how much I wasn't enjoying my own process and then she told me a little story:

So there's this dude in Santa Monica who takes the same bike trail every day. It's an intense workout. He pushes, cranks, and practically kills himself to try to break his personal best time of forty-two minutes out and back. But he can't do it. No matter how freaking hard he kills himself on the trail, he can't beat forty-two minutes. And he's tried and tried to no avail to beat his own best time.

So one day, in a complete change of heart, he decided to screw beating his record and to take his time instead. He worked hard and made the most of his workout but also took some time to relish the ride. He enjoyed the experience, looked around at the immense beauty, and really took it all in. And want to know the time he finished in? Forty-five minutes.

The difference between totally killing himself with misery and actually enjoying this thing he did every day was three minutes. Three freaking minutes.

I know that for elite racers like my Iron(wo)man bestie, Caroline, three minutes is a long time, but this guy wasn't competing with anyone but himself. Nor are you. Your life isn't a race day. Your life is one chance at the human experience—and how much of it do you spend obsessing over hustling hard, striving stronger, wanting more, and being further along? Why destroy your experience for minimal gains?

The experience is the most important result. So take your time. When you give yourself permission to do so, to honor your ascent, genuine enjoyment will follow. The puzzle pieces on the table begin to find their way together once you lighten up a bit.

It's a hard lesson. And most times you don't realize it until you start to become so un-present in your own life that all you do is obsess over finding your path and making shit happen. That is not a life. Let me repeat: That is not a life. Your life is right here, lost and all. The more you take your time accepting that and acknowledging where you're at, the more joy you'll summon back in.

You're on your own timeline, just like most everything and everyone else in life. We can't force creation, but just like you can't talk a baby into being born or a flower into blossoming, it happens when it's going to happen. Magic will reenter your life and clarity of the path will reveal itself as soon as you look up to realize that you're not actually in the totally wrong place. This "wrong" place is telling you everything you need to know about yourself to get into the right one.

★

You've Got This

What goal can you have more patience with? Tell yourself, *I will put in the work, but I will let it take time.*

WHEN A WRONG BECOMES A RIGHT

If you've ever listened to someone who's in the midst of what they consider to be a major misstep, often there's a total lack of self-compassion and plenty of lamenting. It's painful to hear, because all they can do is beat themselves up for what they're doing or not doing. You might even be this person.

If you'd known me early in my career, I was this girl too. I was freaking out about the choices I'd made. Choices that I considered to be totally erroneous. So wrong, in fact, that I mentally placed myself on a voyage to failure, one that I was unlikely to ever return from. But here's the deal with wrong turns: Sometimes you need to make all kinds of them in order to get on the right path.

There's really no such thing as a wrong turn. These are simply steps leading you forward. If only you could pull yourself up for a hot second, you'd see and know that this "wrong" phase in your life is fueling you with information that will eventually allow you to rise, and rise big.

If I'd had someone telling me to chill out, I could have seen that while sports broadcasting may not have been my end-all-be-all calling, I was gaining communication and production skills that I'd eventually use for something meaningful. And I wouldn't have taken for granted for a second the lessons I was learning in management and community development from the retail job that I kept on the side of my low-paying TV gig. All these opportunities that I had deemed "wrong" were planting magical seeds that would sprout later. You're not wrong; you're just learning.

I was reminded of this by an artist who fills my soul with *so* much beauty and inspiration via Instagram. Ashley Longshore is a painter, gallery owner, and entrepreneur based in New Orleans who's anything but your typical sweet-tea-sippin' southern lady. She paints canvases with the phrase *cuntry club* and instead of telling you to grow some balls, she'll tell you to "grow some fucking labia." In addition to being a favorite artist of Blake Lively and building a multimillion-dollar business, she's got a supportive spirit even louder than her art, which shines through her captions and videos draped in f-words and dripping with confidence.

She dropped a few love bombs on me in our chat about letting the rough patches of the journey inform our future steps, and how to love ourselves madly while we do—three lessons specifically that we should all always remember as we figure this out together:

1. Stay Optimistic.

"Even if you're completely in the dark, at some point you're going to see that little pinhole of light. And everything is going to be OK as long as you stay positive. You've got to." Staying positive, she says, can be as small as saying to yourself, "You're OK, girl."

"It's self-love and the constant pep talk. You've got to be your own best coach. You really, really do," Ashley says.

2. The Bad Shit Will Turn into the Good Shit Later.

"Have faith in yourself, faith in humanity, faith. Faith that the right things will happen. Faith that when something is wrong, you're going to come out smarter and better on the other side. This is where that self-love thing is so goddamn important. Slowing down and really honoring the bad shit when things take you off track or throw you for a loop, that's where you get really smart. That's where you learn stuff. That's when you really start sponging and you start thinking, when things don't go right."

3. The Easy Route Isn't the One You Actually Want to Take.

"Let me tell you a story," Ashley said to me. "One morning I woke up and I walked down this road and it was so beautiful and I got to the end of the road. The end."

"Let me tell you another story," she said. "One day I went on a walk down the road. I got fucking attacked by a swarm of wasps. Then all of a sudden a bull came out of nowhere to try to knock me down. I started running, and all of a sudden there were holes on the road. I twisted my ankle."

We can all agree that the latter is far more interesting. Because the good stories are the ones where you learn something. And nothing is ever learned the easy way. "It's not about all this good shit, it's not about Blake Lively, it's not about billionaires, it's not about Ryan Reynolds," Ashley told me. "What it's about is when my ceiling caved in in my studio three weeks ago. That's the thing that makes me smarter. That's the thing that makes me a teacher . . . the bad crap."

I asked her how she gets through the bad days, the ones where we're still in the negative and unfulfilling chapters of our lives. Her answer? "I look myself in the mirror every morning and I say, 'Girl, I love you and I would totally fuck you.' That's how I do it."

You don't always need hindsight to tell you that the hard times are actually priming you. It *is* possible to know that this phase of experience that you so desperately want to be out of is indeed teaching you lessons that you need to know. Believing in yourself means you know—like, really know—that while you don't love where you're at . . . you're acquiring helpful information to whip out later and create some on-point magic. Just keep telling yourself that you've completely fucking got this in the meantime.

Trusting the process is core to trusting yourself. And when you trust yourself, anything ahead is possible because you believe you can. And you will.

> When you trust yourself, anything ahead is possible because you believe you can. And you will.

If you don't trust the process and learn to enjoy this experience, success will always be elusive, whether you're lost or found. Back in those tiny TV-gig-slash-retail-worker days, I'm telling you, I would have lost my whole shit if you'd told me that sooner rather than later I would be living in a magical city like San Francisco, and I most definitely would have cried big grateful tears if you'd also said I'd have a little apartment with amazing energy, terrible tile, and views that allowed me to watch the colors of the setting sun bounce around Golden Gate Bridge every night.

I definitely would have lost my proverbial shit knowing that on the way to running my own business I would spend most of a year living on an island in Indonesia. And I would have wept with relief to know that my entire career is built around speaking with women and getting to witness their journey to greatness while also playing a small part in supporting them on that rise.

I would tell you full out, all out, that *that* would be the greatest exit from the feelings of *lost* that I was currently in. *That* kind of life would be success, done and done.

It's funny then, that sitting here in that very life I once would have fangirled over, I can easily fall into the trap of striving. If you ask me what else I want, I can rattle off a list of ten things I should or could be doing, and I'll rattle them off quicker than you can spit out the question. That list would define success by the world's view of achievement, by culture's constant push for outcomes. But in my heart of hearts, I know better.

I know in that line of thinking, success remains permanently one step ahead of you, and it's wrongly defined altogether, which is why it's so dangerous. If you measure success by your achievement of future goals, then success will never exist, because once you get to the place you wanted to go, you'll already have a higher bar of achievement to meet. Something bigger and better must exist compared to where you're at, even though you are where you once wanted to be. In this scenario, you'll never have what you want, according to your own present judgment.

I don't know about you, but I think that sounds bleak. Luckily, you have full control over whether you fall into this trap. You get to honor where you're at. You get to decide that where you are may not be what you want, but it is serving you, confused . . . anxious . . . wandering . . . lost and all.

Don't let what you desire become an ever-evaporating horizon line. Let it be now.

Perspective can be hard when we're in the thick of things. As the center of your own world, you'll find it's often easier to talk to someone *not* in the midst of your journey about your journey, rather than trying to pull yourself out of it, which feels like scraping up the side of a wall with nothing more than the claws of your own hands. Other people have instant perspective that can help you view your path with a more loving lens. They can snap you back to reality so you can see that where you are ain't so bad. They can help you see that, actually, you're already tap-dancing on the horizon line of success.

★

You've Got This

Take a minute to see your path through someone else's eyes. Ask a human who's known you for a while to tell you their perspective on your path to today. Here are some questions to start:

1. What do you think has gone really right for me on my journey?
2. What areas do you see me excelling in right now?
3. What strengths do you think I successfully tap into the most?

How willing are you to see the goodness in today, in yourself, that they so clearly see?

Hating where you're at gives you an opportunity to declare what you never want again. Confusion is your stepping-stone to clarity. So give it some credit for doing its job. You'll find your direction and you'll reach what you want as long as you don't erase the highlights you've already had from the pages of today.

Otherwise, you put yourself in a position with far more to lose. If you choose not to see your current situation with any kind of positivity, you risk never finding what you want at all. Because you'll always be raising the bar on yourself.

Your direction is nothing more than a decision you make. It's no more than the opinion you have of your work, connections, and creations of today. You get to choose to frame your life and your day as one of *lost* or one of *found*. So look up, look around, and see what's really going on. . . .

WORKSHEET
Take Your Damn Time

You can gain perspective on the present by working to see the full story of your past. This isn't the first time you've waited to find answers and clarity, and it won't be the last.

I want you to remember a time when something you *really* wanted **took way longer** than you'd planned. What was the situation?

What was the **outcome**?

If you had known how it was all going to turn out, **what would you have done differently** while you waited?

If you knew everything was going to turn out just as it's supposed to, how would you treat **today** differently?

WORKSHEET
Seeing Today Through Rose-colored Sunnies

You get to choose how you want to see the events of today. You can jail yourself in feeling lost, or you can liberate yourself by choosing to see the discomfort of today as a lesson. Let this new perspective be your freedom song.

What has been the **biggest challenge** that you've overcome in the past year, and **what did you learn from it?**

★ Do It Now

I want you to imagine your future self looking back on today. What three positive or useful things are you learning the hard way that your future self will be #batshitgrateful for?

1.

2.

3.

Forget the Big Goal (for Now)

*Just don't give up trying to do what you really want
to do. Where there is love and inspiration, I don't
think you can go wrong.*

—ELLA FITZGERALD

THERE'S NO END goal here.

Contrary to basically everything you've ever heard, figuring out where you're going isn't accomplished by having the big picture all sorted out. I understand the insane tendency to emphasize five- and ten-year plans, because not only did I used to be the most invested subscriber of that mentality, I was also an evangelist for the Church of Hyperspecific Goals. I was preachin' and I was believin'.

If you'd met me ten years ago, you would have found someone with highly strategized three-, five-, and ten-year plans that laddered up to the *big* goal, circled in a thick hot-pink highlighter: "Host my own show on ESPN."

Obviously, that's not where my life went. And boy did that nicely formatted goals sheet not work. Here's why: Because it was based on achievement, which has led us *all* astray. When you become completely, utterly obsessed with all of your accomplishments rather than what truly brings you energy, you're putting emphasis on your destination rather than your direction.

Some of the most lost people I've met (my former self included) were queens of the achievement game. They marched their way through their perfectly laid plans and waved at the streets of onlookers with an *I've got this* glow. From stellar degrees to great jobs and big promotions, sprinkled with cool life moments and social-worthy trips, everything was so neatly packaged that when the feelings of discontent set in, it was even more confusing.

But I did everything right. . . .

I should want this. . . .

Am I just totally ungrateful?

Maybe this is just what life is like. . . .

Sound familiar? Achievement is a cotton candy meal that you think will make you full. And the big goal is the wide paper cone that holds the whole misconception, unless you're rooted in why you're really here and what lights you up. That's where everything starts to change—where your hustle meets what inspires you.

This is where lost feelings so often begin—when achievement breaks down and the path is no longer clear. When everything you once desired, you no longer want. When you realize you're not sure you've ever actually known what you want. When the things you thought would make you feel good about life leave you feeling a lot of nothing. It doesn't matter what broke the levy of awareness—you're now faced with a new truth.

And the truth is that you don't know what the next thing is. You don't know where you'll end up or what you'd even write down as that "big goal" if someone put a gun to your head. You don't know where you want to go but you know it's not here. So how do you get out of here if you have no idea where to go?

You've hit the wall most everyone does: the moment when achievements aren't enough to make you feel good, when being busy isn't enough to mask the big questions or to fill the gap between you and the belief that you can do what your heart *really* desires. Somewhere along the way you learned to root your confidence in the goals you've crossed off and the future ones you've written down. But **just because you lose the goal doesn't mean you've lost yourself.** You're simply entering a time of recalibration and rebuilding. You can feel good about yourself and your ability to get what you want without having it all penned out and planned.

Because here's the real deal: Success won't make you happy, but happiness will make you successful.[1] Provided you believe in your core self enough to let go of past goals and to be willing to look your truth squarely in the eye—the truth that has an uncertain path to fulfillment, the one that can't be condensed into one big goal, the one that lights you up so you can radiate with the close heat of confidence.

Recently I was sitting with the girl gang sipping on some weird honey-foam coffee in the back library of a Dallas café.

It's been six years since I moved from this place . . . six years, y'all. It sounds like nothing, but damn does it feel like a lifetime ago.

They nodded in unison, knowing what I meant, fully. Because six years feels like an eternity ago for them too.

So much has changed. I feel so drastically different from the girl who used to live in this town.

More nods as I waxed existential, per usual. And then a question was handed back to me: **But would you have ever seen yourself where you are now?**

Nope. Nope. Hard no. No way. This life I'm living is way more magical than any goal I could have ever set for myself then.

In that moment, I realized how much going goal-less has served me. And how unnecessary far-in-the-future goals have actually always been. Saying it out loud was like taking off a stupidly uncomfortable bra at the end of a long day. Braless is flawless. And so is going goal-free.

Because often, your heart doesn't actually want that end goal, but your head is obsessed. Because it looks good. Because it sounds good. Because you said you wanted it once. If you're being honest, there are *so* many chapters in your life and you're constantly changing within those too. It's important not to resist that reality, and to be willing to embrace a new one openly. So openly.

I also know from experience that realities will show up that are way, way better for the trajectory of your life than some long-term goal list you forced out into your journal one Saturday morning. They're things you couldn't have ever wished for yourself, but they're so, SO much better than anything your past self could have had the capacity to believe in.

So you're going to try letting the goals go, leaving the big picture aside as you walk forward. Goal-less is actually a great place to be. Because it forces you to listen. It requires you to tune in and ask yourself the important questions and pay attention to your deep desires. You feel lost now, but you won't always. What you want is hidden in your heart. We're just going to have to go find her.

One thing you won't be ditching, however, is your desire and your excitement. Not ever.

WHEN MY BIG GOAL BECAME GOD (AND THEN SENT ME TO HELL)

The first phase of my career could have been a manual for Achievers Anonymous. I marched obsessively toward my hot-pink-circled goal, which was a culmination of fifty smaller ones I'd identified as the appropriate stepping-stones to get there. And I took comfort in knowing if I kept on that track then I'd be happy when I finally got there.

Oh, the fallacy of *I'll be happy when*.

But at the time I believed it with everything in my bones, and so the obsessive goal march turned into a choreographed performance on a brightly lit stage. I had not one, but two degrees under my belt. I bypassed my lack of connections with relentless grit and snagged the oh-so-coveted summer sports internship at ESPN headquarters. I clawed my way into meetings with all the top talent executives. I filmed clips for my reel on the set of the NFL Network. I wove in a successful writing gig. And then, finally, I landed the holy grail opportunity for a budding sports broadcaster: hosting a high school football segment in Dallas, my hometown and a top-five news market, with promos for my segment airing all around my town during the commercial breaks of the MLB playoffs.

I was pretty sure I had died and gone to #jobgoals heaven. Everything I'd ever said I wanted was coming together.

It was confusing then, as the months went by and soon I was faced with the reality that in order to continue working in TV, I had to go somewhere smaller and make my big mistakes there. As I sent in applications to local stations, population forty thousand, I felt the air whizzing out of my big red balloon of excitement. And it was exiting faster than I could figure out how to patch the hole . . . because you don't patch helium balloons. You pop them.

Without the glitter of my shiny gig, I found myself questioning everything. Somewhere in the process, the reality of my choices and trajectory had set in.

Did I really want to spend my life covering sports? Did I really care that much about glorified games?

Was I really OK with the fact that my ultimate goal would land me in a city I already knew I didn't care for? (Sorry, Bristol.)

Was this all worth it enough to go and make zero dollars in some small town in order to climb the ladder?

Did I actually want the life that this career required of me?

For a while I refused to contemplate these questions because I was so scared of the answers. I kept myself busy looking for the next "right" step and convinced myself that it was just a matter of finding the perfect new gig. But those questions sat at my feet, waiting to be acknowledged, and refusing, ultimately, to be ignored.

It wasn't until a trip west, in the midst of my *not* wanting to pursue any of the opportunities coming my way, that I was forced not only to look at those questions in my heart, but to really take in what they were asking. And the answers were a big, fat NO across the board.

I didn't want this.

I didn't want where this was going.

I didn't want this life.

The work I'd contribute in my lifetime, I knew in my heart of hearts, was something different, something more, something else.

But I didn't know what that something was. I felt so lost because it's easy to get lost when you don't know why you're going.

A BLURRY BIG PICTURE

When you stop wanting what you once wanted, or when you're afraid to undo all that you have for all that you know to be true in your heart, the big picture blurs out.

And that's OK.

So many people believe that the key to feeling less lost is having a clearer big picture. Not the case. Not the case at all. Because you will not ever think your way to the big picture. If you wait for the big goal to appear and strategize the hundred-point plan to achieve it, you'll always be the kid on the side of the pool waiting and trying to convince yourself to buck up and jump in. The biggest contributor to feeling lost is believing you need to have the end destination completely figured out before beginning.

You don't need an oil-painted big picture or a giant shiny goal ahead in order to gain clarity about your path or feel positive about your ability to eventually figure it out. None of us have a crystal ball telling us what's waiting at the end of the next few decades. But some are willing to start, to restart, to recalibrate their steps despite that. When you're doing something that excites you and resonates with your soul, you'll be more willing to just keep going.

So, just begin. It'll feel unstable and imperfect, but take the steps anyway. And the path will reveal itself to you. The path will unfold. The path and where it's leading will become clear. Until then, it's a blur. Until then, you take action despite the blur.

DITCH THE DESTINATION AND SEEK DIRECTION INSTEAD

Direction is sourced from what brings you energy, from what excites you, what fills you with inspiration. Follow that spark, no matter how fleeting and how small.

Somewhere along the way, you likely looked at the things that excite or energize you and deemed them unimportant because you didn't know where they could lead or you didn't see value in activating those expressions of your own talents. But that was dead wrong. You've got to follow those sparks even when you don't have an understanding of the big vision that they might be leading you to. Many of the most successful people I know started by starting without knowing what it'd all turn into.

When I first met one of the biggest lifestyle bloggers in the game, Carly Heitlinger, I would have told you that she has clearly always known what she wanted to be doing and how to do it. But I couldn't have been more wrong. The path she had created for herself when I met her was *not* anything she had planned.

Her blog, *Carly the Prepster*, started in 2008 from a place of sheer desperation. "I did not start my blog thinking about eight and a half years from now and how my plan was to make this my full-time job, that I'd have a manager, I'd appear in national magazines, speak on panels, and make money," she told me. Nope. She didn't know any of that. She simply knew she had to start.

I call Carly my celebrity blogger bestie because we can't go to breakfast without one of her readers discreetly snapping photos or tweeting about their "Carly sighting." It makes me laugh and simultaneously puts me in total awe that she has built such a loyal and loving community. And I'll add my friend-edits in here that she's not just making money, she's making a *shit ton* of it. But none of this next-level digital success came from a big goal that she passionately backed into.

She didn't start her blog because she had the end dream of wanting major dough, high-profile opportunities, or giant followings. No, she did it because it felt right in a moment when everything else was feeling so, so wrong.

"I was struggling in a horrible way, at the lowest point, feeling like I was *failing*." Around that time of desperation, as she joked with people around her about how maybe the only choice was to go be a toll booth operator, a guy listening suggested she start a blog, because his mom and grandma had one for *The Wall Street Journal*. (This was 2008, when blogging was just barely a thing.)

"I didn't know what I was doing, but I had this strange feeling that it was something that I *really* wanted to be doing internally— that *feeling* that is hard to describe," she said. Hard to describe, easy to recognize, impossible to forget.

She wasn't thinking about anything other than the excitement she felt in that moment of clarity and how to continue pushing it forward. She wasn't worrying about the ten-year plan or the big vision for her blog. She was simply thinking, *This feels right, so let's move.*

"If you are thinking big picture, it's really easy to get discouraged. . . . There's millions of moments of uncertainty, but I do know what I can get done today. I know what I need to do [right now]," she explained.

When everything else felt like it was failing and she had no idea what could possibly be on the horizon for her, Carly followed what felt right even though she didn't know or see a vision of what it could be. All she focused on to get herself from the depths of feeling like a failure was all that she knew: that the idea of blogging and what she'd be writing about excited her. Layer on years of writing, creating a strategic social media plan, lots of business-savvy decisions, and being as sincere as she is fashionable, and within a few years she had the following and success she never knew to dream of. Coming out of her *lost* fog all started with that small feeling of excitement. If you follow your spark, the same can happen for you.

START BY STARTING

The liquid gold in Carly's story is that she just started. She didn't know how to run a blog but she figured she'd need an email address to set one up, so she started there. It seems so simple because it is. Yet we so quickly turn taking action into something way more complicated. And then she just kept going.

Exchanging the exactness of a future goal (i.e., knowing the outcome) for the essence (i.e., doing something that energizes you right now) is less certain, but more promising. Many of us tend to emphasize the former when the latter would have opened up *way* more doors to shift our mindset away from feeling so freaking lost.

Getting *real* clear on what you want to feel and experience requires a little active exploration. And here's why:

- ⤞ Taking action builds your confidence.
- ⤞ Confidence moves you to take even bigger actions.
- ⤞ The right actions are derived from knowing what lights you up. Period.

When you get clear on the *essence* of your desired future journey, you allow the universe to answer with more options than you could possibly imagine. You give your life the gift of wiggle room. You begin to trust your gut instead of muting it with specific goals. Because in this weird life, all kinds of things might show up for you that don't make any sense. They may not be what you said you wanted. But they will *feel* right. And they will feel right because they'll be aligned with the energy of something that lights you up. All of which gets refined and realized through your actions.

A LITTLE PROVOCATION

When people try to help you figure out why you're so lost and stuck, there's an equal amount of *Figure out your future by figuring out your purpose!* or *Just follow your passions!* And I'm even sure it has all tumbled out of my mouth at some point before. But what I know from meeting every one of the brilliant women I've come across in my work is this: If it was actually as simple as that, you would have done it already. And if it was actually the answer, you wouldn't be reading this book.

So I made a vow before writing this to (hopefully) not suck, by reframing some of this lazy advice that has *some* truth to it but is missing its context. And as we know, context is everything.

So let's be real. You and I both know I cannot help you figure out your passions and I don't have the slightest clue what lights you up and why. But I *do* know how to help you peel back the layers and deafening doubt in your head to get closer to the answers. For yourself.

More times than not, a guidepost for knowing where to go next and a foundation block to believing that you can get there is to know *what you feel.* As in what really, really, really matters to you. What lights you up? What are you about? What do you want to stand for in this world? What makes you feel like you're flying even if it's just for a hot second?

Mine? Women's issues. Gender equality. Ultimately, the global rise of women.

And *how do I go about doing that?* A crazy passion for writing, creating, and speaking.

Every day. The end.

But here's the honest truth: It took six years and three careers and countless wrong turns to get to that level of certainty. And to a place where I could make money off of it.

There are moments when I have driven off the cliff of confidence. There was that year my whole body twitched so damn much I was positive that I had a neurological problem. Many tears. Bathroom floor moments. And even now, knowing what I'm here to do, I still have occasional bad days. And I have no idea where this is all headed. But enjoying the journey of this life is easier because I know what lights me up, and most important, I believe that I can act on those things every day.

True confidence requires knowing your sparks. When you don't know, life becomes an ugly rat race for the what. And keeping on that way will put you right on track for an achievement hangover and *lost*-induced confusion.

If you're feeling like *Well, but I don't know what lights me up*, take a deep breath. A long one. Everyone has something that sparks them. It's a matter of unveiling it—then trusting you can do something, however small, about it, which is just a matter of putting what energizes you into action in some small way.

OH, CLEAR AND CONFIDENT ONES

Imagine the most confident person you know. They seem fearless, courageous, and always *so* sure of what they're doing. You feel more alive just by being in their atmosphere.

And more times than not they don't live their life worried about what others think. Being in their presence is like staring at a bright sign that says, DO YOU! And that's how they make you feel, that you can be you and do you. And it's what they do—they listen to their heart and they follow it boldly. They're honest with their trials but not unsure of their decisions. They trust their gut, relentlessly. And even their failures seem to turn into giant life gifts, because you simply forget that once upon a time they tried something that didn't work out. They lift others as they climb and they know *why* they're going. So, they go.

Let me repeat: They know why they're going. And that energy draws you in like a moth to the light. It makes them magnetic, because they're so sure, even if they don't have it all figured out yet, about the value they're here to give. They know the core reason for their future actions.

Why is simply a deep, deep, commitment to what lights you up.

Author and activist Tiffany Dufu is the first person who pops into my mind as the epitome of someone who has designed her life around why she's here (and is a living, breathing lesson in confidence as a result). Luckily, she is one of my dearest mentors, so I've had an up-close and personal observation deck to watch how this is done. The first time I met Tiffany, I felt like I was standing in warm sunshine, even though we were in a dark office corner on a chilly NYC day. She was glowing in her purple dress and I had no idea of the gift that had just walked into my life.

When I asked Tiffany about herself, she said what I've gone on to hear hundreds of times in groups as small as three and as big as a thousand: "The thing you should know about me is my life's work is advancing women and girls. On my tombstone it'll read, 'She got to as many as she could,' and I'm simply project-managing my life backwards."

Truly, I don't even have to go look that up from her bio or the transcripts of our conversation; I can hear her saying it as I recall the lines from my memory. It's as beautiful as it is true. But the most important thing about this is her *dedication* to these things that fuel her soul.

Committing yourself to whatever lights you up is so beyond key, because as it did in Tiffany's journey, from fund-raising to women's leadership to a new start-up to writing a book, if you're in bed with the things that give you energy, you'll trust wherever the journey takes you instead of questioning every step. And most important, you'll trust yourself. You'll have confidence in your steps because you know they're aligned with what matters most to you.

Knowing what excites you, what you care about most, what brings you energy is key to summoning confidence in your life. It's the certainty that will flip your feet out of bed in the morning. It'll be a guiding star drawing you forward when things suck.

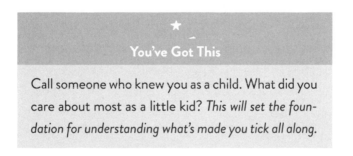

★

You've Got This

Call someone who knew you as a child. What did you care about most as a little kid? *This will set the foundation for understanding what's made you tick all along.*

THE MOVEMENT THAT BEGAN IN MY LIFE

Everything started to change for me when I started my own process of discovering the things that really energized me, and committed fiercely to them. I wasn't at a sexy meditation retreat, closeted within the borders of a faraway continent. Or *ohm*-ing in a forest, surrounded by majestic sequoias. No, I was on the floor of a retail store in southern suburbia.

Seriously. My *aha* moment came while working part time at a lululemon so I could afford my rent. Trying to make that whole TV thing work and survive as an adult got real very quickly. By this time I had already been rubbing shoulders with my own unfulfillment. TV? No. Retail? Nope. What on earth was I doing? Sadly, my crystal ball was foggy as fuck.

During a professional development workshop hosted one early Sunday morning while the store was still closed, I sat and listened to a wise woman decades my senior talk about the importance of a mission statement to ground us in why we're here (not what we're here to do), and I reflected on all the *what*s that had left me empty up to this point. Surrounded by half-dressed mannequins and stacks of yoga mats, she asked us to recall a time when we felt the most alive, proud, and energized. From there we'd pick a few words from the list of a hundred-plus values on a printout in our hands.

None of my current or recent work—the work I had been devoting all of my energy to—came up.

None.

Instead, I thought back to a time years prior, as a journalism student in college, when I was doing what I loved just because. Assigned to write an article for the student sports site, I remember sitting down with a former volleyball teammate, who had lost her mother to cancer in the middle of our season. That sport, our sport, had also been a big part of their mother-daughter relationship. And it continued to be a major piece after her death, a support system and an outlet for her grief.

The hug she gave me after that piece was published is one I'll never forget. I can still feel the warmth of that embrace.

The joy from that simple moment showed me the power for good that words can have. The power of telling women's stories. Writing can connect others to their own story. To their own goodness and possibility. To themselves. (Case in point: You are finding in this very book what you already have inside you.) It lit me up so much, I felt like a walking lamppost. But I wouldn't commit to these things I knew gave me a spark until later—way later, when I basically had no choice.

It wasn't until hitting the depths of my *lost* feelings that I came back to this moment—to the memory of a memory. I didn't think how much writing and women's stories had always meant to me until my life was actually breaking down because I hated my job and I didn't know what was next or what universe I even remotely wanted "next" to be in. When I say I was miserable, I mean I was *miserable*. I was crying a lot. Like, *a lot* a lot. I remember sitting in my car parked in front of Office Depot on the phone with my brilliant mother, sobbing so hard I couldn't talk. Because the little things felt like big things. And I didn't trust myself to make a change. But after one too many basically hysterical phone calls, dinner dates, and borderline anxiety attacks, I realized that I may not know what the final, final thing would be, but I knew what had once made me happy and creative, and no one could stop me from doing that. I'd always had writing, and I would always have it. But I had to do something about that which lit me up. The thing I did next permanently changed the trajectory of my career and my life. And it was a single choice to follow what brought me energy.

That choice was to sign up for a six-week nonfiction writing class at the San Francisco Writers' Grotto (and to fork over more money than my broke twenty-four-year-old self was comfortable with). I arrived to a room of seven *badass* journalists, writers, and creators who were way, waaaay more experienced than I was. When I showed up for that first class, I wondered what I was actually doing there because I was not on a par with these women. But I trusted that through writing, I could eventually share messages about the topics that I felt were aligned with my excitement the most: women, leadership, and careers.

Within a matter of a few weeks, one of the women in my class brought me the front page of the *San Francisco Chronicle*'s business section. On the page was a full-fold image of two women, Amanda Pouchot and Caroline Ghosn, who had started a company based on the same principles I was writing about in that class. "You should get in touch with these women. It might be a great platform for your writing," she said.

I did get in touch with them. And what began as a single, small choice to follow the things that energized me eventually became an opportunity that would turn out to be the rocket ship of my life so far. Amanda and Caroline, the founders of Levo, a start-up designed to support millennial women in their careers, hired me as one of the first employees of their company, and I went on to travel the world, building out their global off-line communities to help elevate women's careers. I got to meet young professional women on the rooftops of Milan and talk about workplace barriers, I got to host negotiation trainings overlooking the London Eye and hear about their insecurities, and in countless cities in between, I was a part of creating a movement for dreamers. And it humbled me. To my core. I saw intimately the challenges and obstacles and fears that we're all faced with. Not only are we not alone, but together, we're unstoppable.

None of these plans were even remotely a part of my original big picture. I never could have dreamt up that dream with all the time and creativity in the world. But it was one of the best things that ever happened for me, and it was all created by following in one small way what deeply energized me.

BOLDLY PURSUE THE SPARK

If you had asked me to define my reason for being during the moments when I felt the most lost, I wouldn't have been able to tell you. A *why*, a *purpose* . . . it all felt too heady. But I could absolutely identify the feeling of a spark. And I do believe we all intimately know what excites us—sometimes you just need someone to come along and ask you the right questions and prompt you to reflect on crucial moments.

We often refuse to go that small because we expect answers to the big stuff—the huge goal, the ultimate destination, the scaled impact. But the only big thing you actually need to know is what gives you the biggest burst of energy.

When I looked back on my life through the lens of what I had been writing about in that class, I realized I had *always* cared about those things. Like, *always* always. I took women's studies classes for fun in college, I performed in *The Vagina Monologues* onstage, wearing five-inch heels and a full-body spandex and leather jumpsuit because #women, I mentored young girls on their résumés and careers on my own time, and I'd never felt more excited and unstoppable than when I watched Sheryl Sandberg's 2010 TED Talk, "Why We

Not only are we not alone,
but together, we're
unstoppable.

Have Too Few Women Leaders." But for some reason I never took the time to identify that this is what was giving me megawatt energy. Because I was too obsessed with hot-pink-circled goals and my sound-goody achievements.

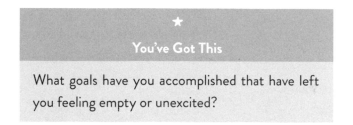

★

You've Got This

What goals have you accomplished that have left you feeling empty or unexcited?

I had never taken the time to question my goal. I'd never asked myself if the same thing that brought me so much joy for no reason at all—like studying, working with, writing about, and engaging around women's leadership issues—was the key to finding direction.

And that direction led me here, to a destination that seven years ago I never would have been able to conceptualize. This life was never an end goal I had in mind, but it's way (waaaaaay) better than anything I had in my list of plans. If you'd described it to me, I would have told you to try again—so dreamy but so not possible.

Following what energizes you will open up the future path for you too. No matter what hell of *lost* you feel like you're swimming through, it's getting you to here. Our lives are changed with tiny decisions led by what excites us the most. Big changes don't always come from big steps. Often, they are born from the tiniest one that we choose to make once, and then over and over and over again.

And they all start with *This just feels right*. That rightness will be summed up in all that you already are, all that you will be, all that you care about, and all that you passionately exist for.

Forget the goal. Follow the energy, follow the excitement, follow the spark. It won't lead you astray. It can't. Because it's you.

WORKSHEET
Find Your Fire

What lights you up? Trust me, it won't come from thin air, but rather from taking an inventory of feelings you've already felt about actions you've already done.

What two things have energized, excited, or inspired you in the past week?

> 1.
>
> 2.

What two things have energized, excited, or inspired you most in the past year?

> 1.
>
> 2.

At what three moments did you feel the proudest of yourself *ever*?

1.

2.

3.

What are friends or family members always coming to you for advice, input, or direction about?

If you could give your time away for free (or maybe you already do), and with no recognition, how would you do so? What would you be doing to make that happen?

★ Do It Now

This week, commit to a single action that gives you that energized, on-fire feeling.

CHAPTER 4

The Big Lie You're Most Definitely Believing

And the day came when the risk to remain tight in a bud was more painful than the risk it took to blossom.

—ANAÏS NIN

WHAT HAPPENS when what brings you energy is something you've never actually pursued before? Well, normally you mutter the common *But I have no idea what I'm doing* phrase. The fear of starting when we don't actually know how or where to begin is a natural one, and it comes with a waterfall of feelings. Because taking on something new, something that we're not sure we're suited for or even capable of, is, well, scary.

And it freaks us out for one simple reason: We don't know yet if we're good at it. Because if we did, we'd probably be doing it already. It's entirely possible we tried once and it didn't go so well.

Shutting off possibilities and options because of your preconceived notions about your abilities is a light-rail journey to mediocrity, to *never* figuring it out. Because here's the thing: One of the biggest lies that you're telling yourself is that your skills are static.

It is what it is. . . . Except it isn't. Because you are a human in constant evolution and so too is everything about you—including what you're capable of.

There's a popular self-awareness zeitgeist around knowing your talents and what you're best in the world at and throwing every inch of your energy into those talents. Listen, I'm the biggest fan of all things assessment, of all things knowing ourselves. Myers-Briggs, StrengthsFinder (now CliftonStrengths), DISC tests—you name it and I've taken it. And then I've gone a step further and championed the awareness they bring, because hi, *know thyself.*

But what about the things you're iffy about, the ones you're energized by but don't feel like you know how to pursue? What about the things you don't give a second look to? What about the paths that interest you, but you've never so much as dabbled in? Well, obviously you're just not meant to take them on because they're not your talents . . . they're not your lane . . . they're not one of your preconceived skills. Right? Riiiiight?

Wrong. But I would have given you a *Hallelujah, so right* had you told me this a few years ago. I would have said you need degrees, you need training, you need education, you need apprenticeship, you need to know your talents and stick with all of them because that's what will get you somewhere. But there's only a fraction of the truth here.

How many times have you heard someone say, "I was really good at what I did but I hated it"? When what you're good at doesn't get you somewhere you want to be, it's confusing and doesn't bring you energy. Often, you'll find your energy and excitement leading your heart somewhere you've only half-been. Just because this isn't one of your self-assessed skills doesn't mean you should turn your back on something that's energizing you.

If I had followed only the interests I was experienced in and had a talent for, there are some major (majorrrrr) opportunities I never, ever would have remotely stepped into—specifically the game-changing ones. There's no way I would have found myself at the helm of Levo, building out global communities and facilitating professional development workshops. There were so many things I didn't know about, let alone know I'd enjoy. I hadn't ever built out off-line workshops. I hadn't ever run them. I hadn't ever created an off-line ambassador program. I hadn't ever worked in women's leadership. I hadn't ever worked in technology or at a start-up. The list goes on.

And besides the specifics of that experience, in general I had always seen myself as a maximizer. I was a self-identified *good-to-great* person, not an ideas-and-future person. Who was I to be building a vertical from nothing? So much of it was not on the list of skills that I considered myself good at.

Not only did I love it, but it turns out I had the chops. And they were the same ones that would later allow me to believe I *could* run my own business and build something personal from scratch. I just had to believe I could learn.

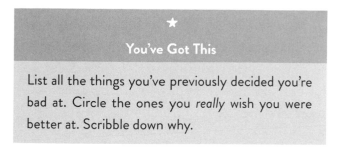

★

You've Got This

List all the things you've previously decided you're bad at. Circle the ones you *really* wish you were better at. Scribble down why.

MAGIC IS IN THE MINDSET

There are numerous problems with obsessing over our talents. It holds us back and seriously squashes our self-belief—unless we choose to get on the right side of our mindset and adopt one of growth.

The term **growth mindset** was first coined by renowned Stanford psychology professor Carol Dweck,[1] and it's a major indicator of confidence because those with a growth mindset know that their skills are a work in progress. They know that just because they're not good at something doesn't mean they never will be. They know their qualities, successes, and talents or lack thereof aren't permanent . . . they're *just not there yet*. A fixed mindset, on the other hand, is where we come from when we think this is just how things have always been and how they're always going to be—that our talents are immovable. And likewise, so are our weaknesses.

I'll never be a good public speaker.

I'm bad at making decisions.

I'm just not a natural leader.

I'm not great at numbers.

I'm not politically savvy.

Strategy isn't my thing.

It's thoughts like these that are oh so fixed. The most successful people take on a growth mindset, which is precisely what it sounds like: a belief that everything has the potential to develop and to grow. Which means those who try on a growth mindset meet natural challenges with optimism and curiosity in order to improve, instead of shutting down and giving up.

MAYBE SHE'S BORN WITH IT?

Or maybe not. At all. It's frustrating when it seems like everything just comes so easily to other people. When we look beyond our path and think, "Damn, everything they do turns to gold. Everything they do happens so easily. Everything they do is a breeze. They're just born with it."

The truth is, by being born, period, you're on the right track. The rest is up to you. You have the ability to take on a mindset that says, *Hey, just because I sucked at this once doesn't mean I always will.* Or *Hey, just because I'm not great at this yet doesn't mean that I can't be great at it later.* Your path in life doesn't always sprout from the God-given talents of the heavens. More likely, your path in life sprouts from your God-fearing determination to stay on it, figure it out, and try to get better come hell or high water.

Writing is my first love. And I've been writing books since my early grade school days at Mathews Elementary, where I first penned "The Magnificent Life of Maxie McCoy" and outlined my future in excruciating detail. I'd like to believe the writing has gotten better (and less prophetic) since.

However, when I first started blogging in 2013—which was born from a desire to capture the conversations with the women I was meeting around the world and these very universal lessons we were experiencing—my shit was shit. And I can barely go back and read those early posts without cringing just a little bit. A part of me so badly wants to hit DELETE on every WordPress post I wrote pre-2015. Every last one . . . especially the one titled "What a Cinnamon Roll Can Teach You About Life." I mean, really? But the other part of me appreciates those terrible public writings as a sign that we can get better at things if we keep showing up. I knew those posts weren't my best then, but I kept putting them out. I kept pressing PUBLISH. I kept searching for my voice. And eventually I found my groove for how to talk about the things I care about, in my own style, with my own swing, and with success. And eventually the validation came.

Which is why, even if that which energizes you, if that which interests you, if that which excites you in the future also comes with equal measures of *but I suck . . . but I'm bad . . . but I don't actually know how . . . but it's shit* . . . you also need to know that that's not permanent. *We're* not permanent. You can and will get better with self-awareness, elbow grease, practice, and a growth mindset.

LET YOURSELF SUCK

Somewhere, somehow, we've done a slippery slide into this idea that our path is predetermined by the things we've previously decided to take on, when, in fact, the future stages of our lives will bring not only new opportunities but also new desires that might be worth exploring. And they'll sure as heck be worth showing up for—even sucking at—and eventually learning from the hard way.

I've done the total opposite of this advice and avoided things like the plague in the name of not sucking. However, holding yourself back because you might be bad at something new is a disaster mindset that only leaves one direction to go: down. The people who eventually do become great are the same ones who are willing to push themselves to figure out their path.

The problem with any of us thinking that our talents, qualities, and even our personalities are fixed is that, according to Dweck, this thinking puts us in an ongoing cycle of having to prove that that's the case *and then attempt to stay static* to maintain that truth. This thinking turns every situation into a confirmation of our greatness, instead of evidence that all of our basic qualities are cultivated through the effort we put into them. Talk about proving yourself gone terribly wrong.

To change your life for the better, you're going to be required to suck, and to become OK with that. It's going to require that you sign up for things that you may not feel you are talented at. It's going to demand that you step out of your lane not once, but many, many, many, many, many times. If you let decisions based on what you were good at when you were fifteen determine the boundaries of where you stay forever, nothing interesting is coming your way. Because that's a coffin of limited possibility that you've put yourself in.

I'm not saying you should leave behind everything you've ever been good at in pursuit of all the things you're shitty at. Nothing can drain your confidence more than having that which you suck at and that which you feel in a groove with totally out of balance. However, progress isn't made in our lives by avoiding suckiness.

For a few years, I'd had it on my list to participate in a poetry slam. Let me first say that my poetry experience is quite minimal, aside from posting short poems on a semisecret Instagram account. My presentation skills and my writing experience are, however, far more robust. But every time an opportunity came about, I found about a million reasons why I couldn't or wouldn't participate. The real reason back then, though, was because *I knew I wouldn't be great right away.*

Great right away? Like, WTF does that even mean? And who on this earth is great right away? Nobody. Well, I'll say *mostly* nobody. I did have a best friend who first picked up a volleyball in high school at sixteen and was a top-ten recruit in the nation by seventeen. So, outliers exist, but most of us have to start somewhere. Yet, that's the expectation we have for ourselves when we step into new things—that we'll be great right away. And it's neither a healthy expectation nor a helpful one.

You have to be willing to dip your toes into the pool of newness and muster some determination to get past the rough patches when you're just beginning. Because your future path will require future skills, and those skills have to start somewhere. And it's most likely not ever going to be on a stepping-stone engraved with GREAT RIGHT AWAY.

Also, where's the fun in that? One of the most rewarding feelings in life is seeing how far you've come, and how far you've come because of the blood, sweat, and tears that you put into something. Practice doesn't make perfect, but it will engage a cycle of perseverance and self-belief. If you care a lot, your effort will come to match the size of your caring, and voilà, you'll make progress.

Here's what I'm not telling you to do: I'm not telling you to go and find a new job you suck at. I'm not telling you to apply for a promotion that you'd be the worst at. *Make your mistakes in a smaller market.* I was told this early on in sports broadcasting. And it's also why so many of us are weekend warriors before that which we love becomes that which we do. Keeping the stakes relatively low when you start your plans for moving forward gives you the space to stretch into new skills. It gives you time to figure out what the hell you're doing and if you even like it. It gives you time to tap into focus and simply encourage yourself by the very act of *doing*. Remember, passions aren't always meant to pay the bills. Sometimes they're just there to keep you creating and moving forward and enjoying your process. Into the creative wilderness. Into the light of something new.

Keep doing what you love and what lights you up not because of any pressure to get it right, but because the practice and focus of it energizes you. That energy will continue to support your outcomes. Seek progress, not perfection.

> **Seek progress, not perfection.**

Years later when a writing festival I attended had an afternoon workshop held by the world's poetry slam champion on the agenda, you bet I signed up. The half-day class finished with poetry presentations from everyone in the class—a mini-slam. You probably know how this ends. . . . I wasn't great, not even close. I did, however, have the time of my life, and acquired a new hobby that fuels my creative-writing soul. And who knows where that will lead?

GET CURIOUS

Part of expanding your skills and your belief in them is dropping the facade of expertise. Our obsession with *experts* has gotten out of control. Because real experts don't call themselves that. Real leaders don't refer to themselves that way. People who are really good at what they do continue to shift and grow because they're obsessed with surrounding themselves with people who are better—way better—in an effort to become better themselves.

Learning begins with curiosity and asking questions. But you can only be curious if you're willing to show the gap in what you know.[2] It requires vulnerability to show that you don't know everything, but it's the only way you'll continue to grow in the things you're trying your hand at.

Ask questions.

Be in wonder.

Be in awe.

Be the last to talk.

Curiosity, that nagging feeling that you'd like to know more or to understand or to follow a feeling a little further, will help you to understand just where your excitements and your energy can lead. So often, though, we write our own selves off—we say that something is silly, or boring, or we wouldn't be good at it.

Instead, let yourself follow that curiosity somewhere. Projects are the long-lost way to do this. They're nothing more than small tests for trying on something new. You don't have to write your life away to a new project. Rather, you could have a weekend project, a side project, or even a here-and-there-when-I-have-time-for-it project. As you dip your toes in the pond curiosity has led you to, ask yourself: How do I feel? How does this project fit my life? Showing a little curiosity and wonder for the world (instead of trying to master it) will take you places you never knew to go. So, always seek curiosity over expertise.

LATE-ONSET SKILLS

There's probably a reason why articles titled some version of "What These 5 Mega-Millionaires Were Doing in Their Twenties" are such viral successes. I can never help myself. I click on them every single time, even though I know they're going to rattle off the same list of people and the random shit they were doing before they became what we know them as today (because that's how life works).

Our society is not-so-slightly ageist, and has led us all to believe that if we're not successful in the first years of our career then we're damned to a failing hell. And these articles go viral in part because they remind us that such an assumption about success is not true. They remind us that success takes time and, more important, that our skills develop, grow, and change.

I've been obsessed with filmmaker Ava DuVernay for a hot minute. She's the director of *A Wrinkle in Time* and *Selma*, and was the first black woman to win the U.S. Directing Award for dramatic film at the Sundance Film Festival. She's major. After watching her stunning documentary *13th* and her interview about the process of making it, I did what I often do with people I'm newly obsessed with—I internet-stalked. For hours. Before I knew it I was crunching numbers from Ava's Wikipedia bio trying to figure out how old she was when she started her own publicity business and then ultimately at what age she first picked up a camera.

Holy shit, I thought. This woman who has created these mind-blowing movies and television that we all know and love today wasn't *always* doing this. She didn't go to school for this. She didn't know her whole life she'd be doing it. Rather, she was in the midst of an entirely different career, noticed the stories being told, and was like *Wait, I could do this.* And so she did. Ava didn't pick up a camera until she was thirty-two, and aspired to be a journalist and a lawyer before any of that.

No, thirty-two is not old. But it's definitely not one of those *I studied this. I'm an expert at this. I've been doing this my whole life* kind of stories. It was an interest, followed by *Why not?* followed by refusing to let a lack of knowledge or experience keep her from trying (and excelling in a monumental way).

Ava DuVernay isn't the only example we have of people picking up skills later in life. And because they were picked up, and committed to, they worked, regardless of whether they were "born to do it" and regardless of whether they were any good at first.

We're talking Vera Wang. Her early skills as a competitive figure skater and journalist are a wee bit different from those of a wedding gown designer, a challenge she took on at age forty. And Spanx founder Sara Blakely, who was a door-to-door office supplies saleswoman before founding Spanx. And hi, Julia Child was in advertising and media before writing her first cookbook at fifty. And then, of course, all those other people on all those other viral lists.

It's not over until it's over. It's not over 'cause you're not on some "Number Under Same Number Age" list. There's no limit to your success and ability to learn something new and make *that* your thing.

MEASURE THE RIGHT OUTCOMES

When you're of the mindset that anything can get better, your confidence also requires that you use your own measuring stick. We do far better when we can manage and recognize our own individual progress, rather than expecting mastery based on predetermined norms.[3] Someone else's path is not yours. Someone else's timeline is not yours. Someone else's outcome is not yours. You have to figure out what progress looks like for you and pay attention to that, rather than beginning something and expecting a specific outcome. That's simply not how it works and will lead you down a rabbit hole of doubt.

Your direction hinges on believing you can get better, and "better" is defined by no one other than you.

So go out there and prove it to yourself.

WORKSHEET
Stalled Out No More

In what areas of your life do you feel *meh* about your skills?

If you had no fear of sucking, which of these would you try to improve?
Write everything that comes to mind.

What's one thing you can do in the next month to try to improve this
skill(s)?

Name someone who could coach you or provide accountability for
improvement.

Setting aside mastery and perfection . . . if progress was the most
important thing, what would that look like to you six months from now for
this area of your life?

★ **Do It Now**

Take one action this week to improve a skill or hobby you desire that you've otherwise determined you're bad at.

Create

CHAPTER 5

That Ride-or-Die Girl Gang

*Abandon the cultural myth that all female
friendships must be bitchy, toxic, or competitive.
This myth is like heels and purses—pretty but
designed to slow women down.*

—ROXANE GAY

O N YOUR JOURNEY to finding your way, there's nothing more powerful and more needed than a community. None of us can rise to the top alone. And we're growing up and building a life at a time when the expectations for our relationships among women are as high as the depth we expect from those friendships. It's less about catty shit where evening cocktails are filled with the latest gossip and more about lunches that turn into dream-brainstorms because you just can't help but be excited for where your gal pal is going.

The women in my life have always seen, clearly, the next steps on my path before I have. **What I learned is to start believing them sooner.** When your friends expect big things of you, and vocalize what you're capable of, it only makes sense that that energy will naturally draw you forward in that direction. It's why I am where I am today.

I once heard a sentence that summed up the deep appreciation I have for my girl gang: "Your success is a direct correlation to the expectations of your peer group."

And it's true. So true. If you surround yourself with people who believe in all the best parts of you, if you spend time with people who cheer you every step of the way, who tell you that you've got this, who expect nothing less than total empire building, and who pick you up with a big hug and coffee date when you're in a funk, there's nothing that can stop you. *Nothing.*

I haven't always had a girl gang of mind-blowing women who I called friends. In fact, my younger years were drastically different. I navigated the treachery of school, trying to fit in, trying to look the part, trying to do my thing, trying to stand out but for none of the wrong reasons. I had a group of friends, for sure. But my friends were only great until they weren't great to me. And the latter is all that actually matters. I had episodes here and there of being picked on, being bullied (by my own "girl-friends"). I've never experienced Monday-morning scaries worse than the time my "friend" group called from a party over the weekend to say some awful things, laugh in unison on speakerphone, and remind me of the invite I didn't get. They knew it'd hurt. And it did. Years later some of those same girls (don't ask me why I kept them around) would finally push me to my friendship breaking point when they shut me out and ignored me relentlessly.

Luckily, I was born into a circle of women who loved me fiercely. Between my sister and my mom, the original girl gang had my back. I think my mother had endured one too many fed-up months watching these girls treat me like shit. So, in the middle of high school, just before I could drive, she picked me up and handed me a pamphlet for

International Baccalaureate, an academically rigorous program that would allow me to take my studies to another level, set myself up well for the colleges that I had my eye on, keep my varsity sport eligibility . . . and, oh yeah—change schools. "I already called. They said you can start in the fall," my mom told me as I looked over the pamphlet. This wasn't a totally new option—it's something we'd discussed prior—but I hadn't wanted to change schools in the middle of high school. But now, with friends who were acting like anything but, it felt like my saving grace.

So I did it. To get the hell away from girls who acted more like a gang of bullies than a nest of support. And with that decision, on the first day of stepping foot on that new high school campus, I met a new bestie, Kathleen. You know that one friend that opens up an entire other world of friendships, opportunities, and life experiences? That was her. From high school to club volleyball to college besties to postcollege gal pals, her friendship introduced me to other friendships that would go on to change my path for the better and will most definitely span many more decades to come. Kathleen showed me the power of supportive and uplifting friendship. At the time, it was a stark contrast to what I had experienced, and I vowed not to make space for anything less than that again.

Nothing has changed the course of my life more than the women in it. And it's taken a lot of years, some negative experiences, and some incredible ones to get it right. And it's important that we eventually do get it right. Because yes, friendship is obviously nice and necessary to our lives, but it's also way more integral to our confidence and to blazing our path than we might give it credit for.

Many years later, heading into the speakers' dinner for Create &

Cultivate (a conference for creative and entrepreneurial women), I wasn't thinking about snapping a picture, or cursing the business cards I'd forgotten to stuff into my clutch (or even worried about the sweat stains that were surely creeping onto the armpits of my rose-colored dress). The women in this room must have had half a billion followers combined, so I probably should have cared a tiny bit (about the biz cards, at least). But I didn't. All I could focus on was how freaking *jazzed* I was to see some of my dearest friends.

Because in this room was my girl gang—the women who continually give wings to my rise. As I got seated, I realized how many of these ladies had had a direct impact on my life and my belief that nothing could stop me—especially two women there, Jaclyn Johnson, Create & Cultivate's founder; and Carly Heitlinger, who'd arrive soon. They are two humans, specifically, who've been some of my greatest cheerleaders and peer mentors, and whom I owe a shit ton of my business success to.

Jaclyn has owned and sold multiple businesses, not to mention created one of the coolest brands for women who want to take over the world. First off, she hustles so damn hard and stays funny and kind while she's at it. She's the warmest kind of fierce and goes all in for the women in her life. Luckily, I get to be on the receiving end of that support (and try to give it back, as well).

I first met Jaclyn when we were planning the biggest event Levo had ever taken on: bringing Sheryl Sandberg to NYC for an exclusive event planned by Jaclyn's agency for the community we'd built at Levo. We were all in over our heads. But though we were nervous and unpracticed, we were also smart and ambitious and we pulled it off—big-time. Fast-forward a few years and Jaclyn invited me to moderate a morning panel at Create & Cultivate, her conference series, in Chicago, which was followed by hosting panels, emceeing the stage, and hosting mentor circles for the cities to follow. In each of those cities I've had the opportunity to build and deepen life-giving friendships with other women invited to be there. It's a gift that keeps on giving.

Jaclyn is always the first person to pull me over to meet women at the helm of top brands who are looking for talent like me. She doesn't simply say, "Meet Maxie," and move on; she takes the time to describe why she believes in me and how I add value to the women around me. These introductions have turned into everything from lucrative business opportunities to life-changing friendships.

When I asked Jaclyn why she is always *so* supportive of me and others, she explained that she wants to give other people what she didn't have. As a nineteen-year-old who'd moved to NYC not knowing a soul, she fought tooth and nail for every job, introduction, and opportunity she got. So the people who answered those cold-call emails or offered her help, they stuck with her. She promised herself then that she'd be one of those people when the time came and she had things to give back. "I will forever want to be connecting cool people, interesting people, and wanting to make other people money because that's what you should do," she said.

When Carly, who you were introduced to earlier, got to the dinner, we sat together immediately. The night she and I first met, we were colleagues and ended up having to sleep together in this tiny hotel-room bed in Boston. I'm not sure either of us knew at the time how that one weird situation would blossom into a beautiful friendship. I sure didn't. I also didn't know that I'd just met the woman who'd first break open the door of possibility for me down the road.

Because Carly had been running her supersuccessful blog for years before I started writing on my own site, she sat me down at one point to show me the ropes. She told me I needed traffic and promptly suggested I start guest-blogging for her site to get it. My twice-monthly guest posts, "Maxie Mondays," were born, as was the opportunity that would put me on the internet's radar. Suddenly, I had a following, one I'd be able to layer and build a business upon. "I wanted you to succeed. Who wouldn't want that? The more successful you are, the more successful I am," Carly told me later. And she's right. So right.

> **Your people want to support your success. And if they're not supporting you, they're not your people.**

Your people want to support your success. And if they're not supporting you, they're not your people.

Even if you don't have that superconnector friend like Carly or Jaclyn, that doesn't mean you can't take leaps forward in oh so major ways. You just have to look for people who are around you, instead of ahead of you. "Don't necessarily seek out the most successful people right away to be in your circle. Go with the girls who are in the same grind as you are," Jaclyn explained, to which I say *amen*. Those in the same stage in their hustle will be able to help you from exactly where you're at. They'll be much more accessible, and together you'll all grow over time. Your success will be their success and vice versa.

Surround yourself with people who believe in you, people experiencing your experience, and *verbalize* your encouragement for each other. It's a practice that you should get in the swing of—to remind each other of your awesomeness and then pay it forward every chance you get in terms of opportunities. If that's not something your girls currently do, there's no better time than now to lead by example.

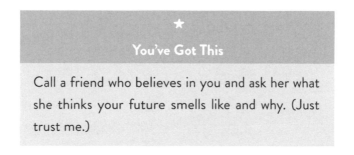

★

You've Got This

Call a friend who believes in you and ask her what she thinks your future smells like and why. (Just trust me.)

In the moments when I've felt the most confused about where I'm going and the *least* confident in my ability to ever figure it out, the girl gang has always come in hot, firing on all cylinders. They always do.

In the late summer of 2014 I had hit one of these moments. By this time, I knew the things I was most energized by were eventually taking me somewhere *other* than running the global Local Levo communities. But I didn't believe that I could ever build my own business or that it could become my "next step." It felt right, but I was scared shitless because I loved my current job while also feeling a deep call to do something more.

During this specific time of confusion (which was really just a lack of confidence to follow my gut), I remembered an article I had saved a few weeks prior while waiting for my plane to take off from

Heathrow Airport. Those international flights always take a super-long minute to get everyone on board, so I had time, lots of time, to review Gina Bianchini's many opinions on building a personal brand (i.e., the way others see you). Gina is an investor and tech leader in Silicon Valley, and I was lucky to call her a mentor, one who taught me much of what I know about building communities online. Her article included a suggestion to outsource a survey to your friend so they can talk to the people closest to you—a recipe for more honest feedback, she noted.

I texted the link to a friend, Meaghan, because I thought she would like it, powered my phone down, and didn't think much about the article until about three weeks later, when the *but where am I going?* feeling bubbled up again, and hard.

Turns out, Meaghan had been feeling the same draw toward something else, so we made a pact to conduct Gina's survey (or a version of it) for each other.

I didn't know then that the answers would change my life. And they still bring tears to my eyes as I write this.

There's a funny thing about truth that resonates with your soul—you can't unsee it. And as soon as you start to see yourself through the eyes of those who love and believe in you, it's like opening up a portal to realized potential. Which is why it matters that you build a girl gang around you that is proud to know you, willing to challenge you, inspiring, and a whole hell of a lot of loving. When you find those like-minded humans, invest in deepening those relationships, and hold them close.

DNA OF A GIRL GANG

I've thought about the different roles of the women in my girl gang that have been so necessary over the years, because people ask what they should be looking for when building theirs. Here's my fifteen-person girl gang roster so you can keep an eye out for them in your own life. One of the greatest investments you can make in your future is in the women who will get you into action *today*.

Remember, relationships are everything. As you read through these descriptions, there's a space to write the first person in your life who comes to mind (and yes, you can repeat people throughout this exercise; there's no right or wrong here). **Remember, if no one comes to mind, it's totally OK! Really. Do not judge yourself here. We'll figure out how to fill in the gaps later on.** This is simply a tool to see what support systems might be missing from your treasured girl gang.

1. **The Manifester:** We all need help with our dreams. And some people are really good at lighting a candle when you need it most. Just knowing you have someone on your side to send up some wishes will remind you that there's more support around you than meets the eye. Find someone who has a special skill for helping you see your own strength and supporting your dreams so that they come into reality quicker.

   My Manifester:

2. **The Triumphant Contemporary:** I've been graced with too many of these to count. This is the bestie who's killing it—likely, your most successful friend or the peer who shows you the

ropes. You want a friend who is going to be more excited about your success than you are, because she has enough of her own.

My Triumphant Contemporary:

3. **The Mentor:** Mentors have landed me every major break I've ever had. From writing gigs to TV spots to team tryouts to promotions to an agent. They get you where you're going. They leverage. They call you on your missteps. And they're as willing to learn as they are to give, thus allowing a beautiful two-way street of information, love, help, and genius.

My Mentor:

4. **The Coach:** Because of a coach, I had help creating a strategy to go to Bali and stay there for months. Because of a coach, I've been able to hire people onto my team. These are the friends who are not afraid to give you feedback and help you get to the insight that will lead to your own personal breakthrough.

My Coach:

5. **The Energizer:** This is the person who fills you to the brim with positivity, light, and *oh so inspired* energy. She's the person you leave skipping, truly skipping, after being in her presence. This might be one person or it might be your whole girl gang. Pay attention and keep close those who fill you. And always try to be an Energizer in return.

My Energizer:

6. **The Recharge:** Who do you feel comfortable with when you're running low, feeling the yellowy orange of power-saving mode? Who can you let down all of your guard with and not have to "act" in front of? Who lets you recharge when the rest of the world wants your energy? And a little lesson learned the hard

way about these people: While they hold the space for you to be drained, they deserve your best too.

My Recharge:

7. **The Cuppa:** This is the person who you can have endless long talks with about shit that just doesn't matter, and even longer talks about everything that does. She's both your hot-tea-until-it's-cold-on-the-couch person and wine-nights-that-leave-you-with-a-massive-hangover-and-an-even-happier-heart person.

 My Cuppa:

8. **The Believer:** They believe in everything you are, what you've done, and what you still have left to do. They don't flinch when you stumble and they don't blink when you screw up; rather, they're always one to extend a hand to get you back where they know you want to be. They believe in humanity and they believe in you and, more important, your reason for greatness.

 My Believer:

9. **The Spark:** They are a quick strike of energy that gets everything moving—the ideas, the creative frustration, the introductions. You can always turn to them to kick-start momentum because they're great at knowing what to say to get you to begin.

 My Spark:

10. **The Love:** Everybody needs epic love. Friends are so, so good at laying on the love when we need it most. This is the person always flowing with love regardless of what's going on. She can deafen your pain with a single bear hug and return you to yourself when you need it most.

 My Love:

11. **The Sister:** Sibling or not, this woman knows you and believes in you, *fiercely*. She's the one who you can pick up with weeks later. She's also the one who never fails to call you on your shit. She'll answer the phone in the middle of the night. She'll make you laugh in the face of tears. She'll key that asshole's car. She'll look at pictures of the rash on your butt and attempt to diagnose it from eight thousand miles away. And she'll always share her wine.

    My Sister:

12. **The Planner:** They just get things going. They're the friends who'll send over a mean spreadsheet template when your budget needs a refresh, or they'll forward their contract template for you to copy when you start your consulting business. They're always planning fun trips or nights out, yet they give you structure where you need it and keep you committed to progress.

    My Planner:

13. **The Mystic:** This is that superexistential friend who is always reminding you that none of this really matters and that we're a part of something so much bigger. She gives you reason to hope and reminders that your thoughts are creating your reality. The Mystic will geek out with you on the #universe and quantum physics, and brings you out of the bullshit and the day-to-day to dream big, see bigger, and understand that our interconnectedness goes far beyond this life.

    My Mystic:

14. **The Anchor:** In their presence you'll always feel at home and want to stay there when life gets crazy and things go awry. In their presence you remember that none of this is really that bad and that, indeed, this too shall pass.

My Anchor:

15. **The Strategist:** This is someone who's *really* good at helping you see four steps ahead to make a decision about what to do right now. She can beautifully pull out the answers that you already have inside you and help you see what you already know.

My Strategist:

Whether you have some vacancies or none at all, knowing who is in your corner and who you've yet to find will make an impression on tomorrow as much as it does on next year. If your list is full and brimming, tell these humans what they mean to you. It'll deepen your friendship. We never share our appreciation *enough*. If your eye is on those open spots, know that **just being aware of what might be missing is enough to begin attracting that person to your life.**

But if you're ready to be more than aware, here are some quick ideas (all of which have worked in my own life) for building a more robust group of women friends that feels equal parts soul sister, support system, and fun factory:

Ask for introductions: When I moved to San Francisco and knew only two or three people, my (eventual) friend group came mostly from long-distance friends who introduced me to their people in my city. Like typically attracts like—there's a pretty good chance you'll hit it off with your friends' friends. You just have to ask.

Find a like-minded networking community: I can't keep track of how many lady friendships were born from the Local Levo communities we built—for me too. When you bring like-minded, socially conscious, intelligent women together, friendships are a natural offshoot. So look for a networking group that feels right to you and see who you meet.

Take a class: Surface-level events like happy hours can be hard for really getting to know someone. Classes, however, allow you to focus on a specific interest while getting to know the people around you. It's fun and the pressure is off. And bonus, you get to learn *and* connect.

Reach out on social: I met a dear friend, Lauren, on Twitter because I reached out in the DMs. We were working in similar professions at the time and happened to be going to the same conference that month. It's a friendship I still treasure all these years later. If you seem to have mutual interests, try reaching out with a specific ask—you never know!

Whatever you do, if you're in a place where your life could use more supportive relationships, you've got to *try*. Look for people who you just click with, and then make some follow-up effort. Sometimes these friendships will find you, but most times you'll find them. Needing that girl gang is nothing to be embarrassed about or ashamed of. If you honor the need, you'll create the solution.

> If you honor the need, you'll create the solution.

ONE SURVEY, ONE GIANT LEAP

When Meaghan and I initially executed our personal branding survey pact, I thought it was simply a fun exercise that might lend some insight into my next step.

I didn't know that the exercise would do way more than that, not only identifying exactly what that next step should be, but giving me the courage to take it.

Though it's not popular to say, you *can* often develop your confidence with the external validation of others. They think you can, so you *can*. They think you will, so you *will*. They believe in you enough to get you started until eventually, you believe in yourself enough to keep going. That external validation is an important piece of our own belief in ourselves.

Early on I told you that no opinion, judgment, or cultural message should keep you from being fully you. However, the external validation that we're talking about here is reinforcing everything you already are and helping you to see that greatness; it's not about asking you to change anything. That's the difference (and an important one at that).

That's why the right girl gang matters so much. That's why it's essential that they fiercely believe in you. Because eventually, with the help of their encouragement, you'll take enough actions and enough steps in the direction of your dreams that you begin living the life they once told you was possible. (And hopefully you can do the same for them.)

That's where I am today, and it started with the results of the survey of about twenty of my closest humans, most of whom were friends from my girl gang. Response after response, all uttered versions of the same thing: You're the only one holding yourself back from creating the exciting future we all see so clearly for you. They identified the talents that I needed to magnify: supporting women, encouraging people's dreams, rocking stages and cameras, and elevating an audience.

Their answers would launch me into one of the wildest changes of my life, and the gateway to everyday fulfillment.

I didn't know if I could do it, but I believed that *they thought I could*, and oftentimes that's enough. Today, my belief in myself finally matches their unrelenting confidence in me.

THE REFLECTION YOU NEED: YOUR OWN PERSONAL SURVEY

There's not a right or wrong way to do this, but focusing on getting the right energy from the right people is important. You *don't* want to send this survey to the person in your life who always seems to undercut your success.

When I sat down to think about the humans I wanted to ask about how they perceive me, I jotted down the people who loved me hard and believed in me even harder. It was everyone from family members like my parents and siblings to the girl-gang humans who are always so giving with their articulate thoughts and never cease to *just get me*. I also included a few people I considered more mentors or sages.

So here's what you're going to do. . . .

I want you to call up the friend from your girl gang who just *gets* this stuff. She's probably the best friend you're always big-sky dreaming with. You're going to give her the email addresses of fifteen to twenty-five people who love and believe in you. Think about old bosses, friends, mentors, coaches, advisers, besties, family, and so on.

Tell her to put them all on BCC and send an email that goes something like this one Meaghan sent out for me:

From: Meaghan Barbin
Date: Sat, Jul 26, 2014 at 10:05 PM
Subject: Maxie Needs Your Input!
BCC: All the humans

Hello Dear Friends and Supporters of Maxie,
    I'm reaching out because Maxie has asked me to run an anonymous personal branding survey for her.
    As we all know, it can be difficult to give and receive feedback when something is as personal as our own brand. It's important that she has a better understanding of how she's currently perceived in terms of talents, value, and your ideas of how she can continue to evolve. She really values your opinion, which is why she's asking you for help.
    Please fill out this survey, which will take no longer than 10-15 minutes, by August 1. I'll be aggregating the feedback for her anonymously and she'll have no way of attributing responses!

Best,
Meaghan Barbin

Gah, she's such a good friend, isn't she? I'm still thanking her for it to this day, just like you'll be thanking your friend. So pick a friend you're cool owing everything to for, like, ever.
    The questions we asked were iterations of Gina's original article about personal branding, with a few spiced-up questions of our own.

Feel free to do the same, but generally, it should look something like this:

The five questions we used:

1. What makes Maxie irreplaceable?
2. What is Maxie's superpower?
3. If there's one thing holding Maxie back, what do you think it is and how could she improve on it?
4. When you imagine what Maxie is up to five years from now, what do you see?
5. Any additional notes or sleepy thoughts on Maxie's personal brand, talents, unique value, potential, etc.?

You can use any of the survey tools out there, like Google Forms, SurveyMonkey, or Typeform, which will all aggregate the responses in a single spreadsheet. Then, have your survey partner in crime synthesize the responses, delivering it to you verbally and lovingly first. Then have her follow up with the raw answers.

When I got my answers, I was overwhelmed, emotional, and unsure of how to digest their confidence in me:

"I see Maxie on TV. Maxie launching a new book. Maxie running her own consultancy, show, or some form of media."
"Some key words related to Maxie: unique, women, thrive, communication, people, life, future, emotion, potential, happiness. She has an amazing talent for writing and communicating."

"I see Maxie running a Marie Forleo–style company, teaching women to build the businesses, communities, and lives of their dreams."

"Maxie's superpower is her ability to emotionally connect with anyone on the planet. And to talk about things that are usually uncomfortable or off-limits in a loving, inclusive, connected way."

Over the days and weeks that followed, I started to believe what they were seeing, which I proved by taking action. And I could see my next steps because in one way or another these responses gave me the energy to do the small things I had already been thinking about deep down. Soon, launching my own business writing and speaking to women didn't seem like some kind of crack-pipe dream.

Within a month of doing this exercise and taking a trip to Denver, which you'll hear about later, I was ready to initiate the conversations that couldn't be undone. The conversations with my parents, my bosses, my roommates, and my friends that said: I'm leaving my job and life as I currently know it and I'm going to take the first steps in creating a business that might just be viable.

Within three months of this survey exercise I had booked a one-way ticket to Bali.

And within ten months of this exercise I was in the loft of a new San Francisco bar filled with the same girl gang who'd answered these questions, toasting the launch of my business. Because of them. Because of this.

When you complete this exercise you'll have just as many light-bulb moments ahead of you. While your path will look completely different from mine, ideas that you've previously suppressed might bubble their way up. Let them simmer and when you get the hint of a feeling about how to act on the idea, *do it*. It may not be as major, it may not be as drastic, but it will be the small step now that you look back on and see was *the* giant step all along.

AS DEEP AS THE OCEAN

It takes a really good friend to take time out of her crazy week to comb through the responses of people she likely doesn't know to help you see what she sees, what they see. But these are the deep relationships that will get you moving. This is the girl-gang material that will give you a spark to keep making tiny decisions that feel right. You're climbing up the mountain of your life, but you're not doing it alone.

> There's nothing more powerful in our lives than a circle of supportive women.

I believe there's nothing more powerful in our lives than a circle of supportive women. The one that forms around the kitchen while you're waiting for those pot stickers to crisp and solving each other's problems. The circle created from a group hug at the airport after months of not seeing each other, making life feel alright again. And sometimes, the one orchestrated by smart event organizers who know that putting fifteen like-minded powerhouses in a circle around each other can create the most epic mentorship moments for everyone.

That's what I was doing, leading a mentor power hour at Create & Cultivate, the day after that speakers' dinner with Jaclyn and Carly.

During a half hour of people throwing questions my way, one of the young women asked me how I usually landed my speaking gigs, brand partnerships, press, and big opportunities. I hadn't ever verbalized where all of my success came from, but my lightning-quick response showed just how sure I must have subconsciously been about this all along: *Deep relationships with women who believe in me.* Period. The end.

You know those steps that permanently alter the course of your reality? Maybe it was the person who first did the introduction to that coveted internship you got in college. Or the friend who threw your name in for that role opening up. Or the one who took you through a mock interview. Or who helped you whiteboard the hook in your writing because you were panicking.

For me, I can trace every spike in my confidence to the women who believed in and vouched for me way before I had the capacity to do it myself. I told the girls sitting around that mentorship circle about my first five-figure partnership deal and how it had come from a woman who saw my potential and pitched me to her agency.

There are many, many other examples in my personal life, as there likely are in yours. And you can create more.

I can assure you that while I was making those friendships I simply saw something in those women that inspired me, and luckily they were open to developing a relationship with me because there was something in me that inspired them.

That's the magic. But it only works if you are willing to give back in equal measure. I support my girl gang with words and with actions. I remember. I offer my connections and paint them handwritten cards every New Year. I shout about their success on Facebook, acting like their personal PR rep any chance I get. I'm reminded with every ounce of belief they send my way that I'm on the receiving end of the greatest gift: their confidence in me. And it's up to me to do something with it.

While forming deep relationships also sounds like great networking advice, it's more important for you to see that keeping the gang of girls who really get your talents and see you—like, *really* see your value—will help you usher in new phases and next steps that eventually open up your path in a big way. And so much of being seen by others is being willing to expose your vulnerabilities, to ask for help and to be raw with them. Nobody can build a meaningful friendship with a perfect plastic doll. They want a real human. So show up as your full, most expressed and imperfect self and let them really connect with and love that person, not the one in your well-filtered photos.

These friendships will require you to show up. They'll require you to try. You've gotta be in the business of building the relationships you hope to have in your life, and deepening the ones you want to keep. It's one of the most worthwhile investments you can possibly make. Because when you're propped up by their continuous support, you'll find direction faster than if you tried to navigate this entire thing on your own.

So, lean on them. You won't be feeling like this forever, and when the tables turn one day, you'll have the opportunity to be the rock they so badly need.

WORSHEET
Get That Girl Gang

Part I: Taking Inventory
In order to build out your girl gang, you've gotta take inventory of where you already are. Figure out who energizes you (and who drains you).

In the past month, who were the three people you hung out with, talked to, or met with who left you feeling high on life—like you could accomplish anything?

1.

2.

3.

What two people just "get" you?

1.

2.

When something great happens, which gal pals are more excited about your success than you are?

When you feel like the fullest expression of yourself, who are you with?

Which of your friends do you talk to about ideas, dreams, and goals (rather than talking about other people)?

Now take the people who showed up in your answers from above and compile them into one list. Whether these people live halfway around the world or right next door, these are the relationships to cultivate, focus on, and give attention to. These are the relationships that will be the foundation of your girl gang:

Your Energizer List

If there are friends in your life who you're always around but who do not show up on this list, make a mental note. It's up to you to minimize time with these people or to change the nature of your relationship. Try talking about more meaningful topics. Try sharing your success. Try asking about theirs. If over time this doesn't work, you may realize that this friendship doesn't align with what matters most to you and is not a good fit for your girl gang.

Part II: Attracting New Friendships

No matter how strong your girl gang is today, there's always an opportunity for new relationships that make your confidence come alive and help new realities become possible.

What three things interest you the most?

> 1.
>
> 2.
>
> 3.

What's one action you can take in the next month to engage with people with similar interests?

>

Who is one person you've wanted to meet, either from mutual friends or social stalking?

Assignment: Reach out to them for coffee or a Skype date.

Part III: Deepening Your Girl Gang
The beautiful energy you're getting from your girl gang is a direct reflection of the support and energy you're giving back. It's important to think about how to be there for them.

What are three major life moments coming up in your girls' lives?

Think new jobs, big pitches, moving in with partner, moving homes, etc.

1.

2.

3.

Now add these moments into your calendar and shoot them a love note when the day comes. Little messages can mean the world.

Shoot out an email or group text to your girl gang asking what they need help creating or overcoming in the next month. Tell them you'll be sending up some major prayers or energy on their behalf. And then do it.

CHAPTER 6

Ritualize Your Highest Potential

You are your best thing.
—TONI MORRISON

WHEN I OPENED THE BOX that had shown up at my doorstep, I howled with laughter and surprise, "OPRAH?!" In my hand was a tall devotional candle like the ones lining old Catholic churches, typically adorned with one of their many saints.

Not this candle. This one had Oprah Winfrey Photoshopped into her most pious and saintly self, with a bright light-streaked heart at the center of her chest. Saint Oprah. It was a fitting gift from a friend who has heard me joke one too many times to actually be kidding that Oprah is my religious experience.

Before I knew it I had burned through numerous Oprah candles.

Need some support? *I'll light Oprah.*

Worried about that interview? *I'll light Oprah.*

Freaking out about the future? *Girl I've got you; I'm lighting Oprah.*

It became my go-to ritual for activating my wishes and my support—for friends, for family, and for myself. There's not a day I sit down to write that she's not flickering in the background. Something about it made me feel emboldened. So I kept doing it, lighting up this crazy candle whenever I was having a hard time mustering confidence in an outcome. It's my thing. Light her up and think I can. Light her up and know I will.

Rituals, no matter how wacky or simple or weird or common, have a way of connecting us back to the power we know is within and around us. And when you need energy to believe in the actions ahead of you, to remind you that forward is not as hard as it seems, a ritual can do just that.

Before your mind goes wandering off into voodoo religious land, know that a ritual is simply any repetitive behavior that you do with an intention to feel how you want to feel. The word actually originated from the Sanskrit *rtu*, meaning "menses"—that is, something that happens cyclically. A ritual can be a carriage for positive and powerful feelings of confidence, ones that allow you to pursue your future. Because your path isn't going to just pop out for you, your small, day-to-day routines are like the fuel that will keep you moving forward in the face of uncertainty. And it's up to you to integrate rituals into your life intentionally that help you keep going. Always keep going.

FIRST THINGS FIRST

If I asked you to jot down ten things hovering on your to-do list like a horrible helicopter parent, I'm pretty positive you could give me twenty. Because there's always so much shit that has to get done. And there's even more that we'd like to get done, sprinkled with a few things we wish we could focus on. It's never ending. For any of us. For all of us. If there's one collective experience most of us surely have, it's the to-do list.

But think about that list—are *you* anywhere on it? I'm sure there are emails and errands and work and chores and phone calls and—oh shit—that shirt that's been chilling at the dry cleaner for, oh, weeks. But is there anything on this list that brings you energy, gives you joy, and fills up the fuel in your tank? Or do you always get pushed to the bottom, per usual?

The things that bring you energy cannot be labeled as "nice to have if there's time." They must be a must-have, and prioritized, and put first, and scheduled the same way you would a meeting with a boss. You've *got* to be number one on your to-do list.

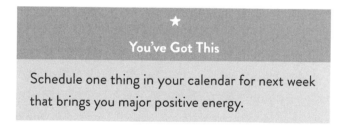

★

You've Got This

Schedule one thing in your calendar for next week that brings you major positive energy.

As I was growing up, my wonder-woman working mother always took a bath before bed while drinking a big glass of milk (and still does). It was something that always just seemed a part of my reality, something I never questioned nor even realized she did every night. It wasn't until recently that my sister and I brought it up to her: "You seriously take a bath *every* night. Like, every night? No matter what?" we asked. She smiled as she said yes, but it was the kind of smile that said, *You seriously are both just now noticing this, three decades later?*

Raising four wild children, keeping a household together, and running a business with my dad didn't leave a lot of daily self-care time. So she worked with what she had and turned her bedtime into a ritual to bring calm and peaceful energy back into an otherwise hectic routine.

My mom knew then what it took me a long time to figure out: The best self-care is simple, like infusing something you already do (like bathing) with intention. Contrary to what the seven hundred gemstone candles, bee-venom-infused facial masks, and luxurious workout studios you see daily on social media tell you, putting yourself first doesn't have to require a massive bank account or a ton of time.

We live in a cultural moment that puts a *lot* of emphasis on the self. Like, loads of it. In the world of women there are a million messages about how we must put our life vest on first before we can help other people. Somehow, what is a rock of truth has been twisted into a rationale for obsessing over the care of your own wellness and well-being while ignoring what's happening in the world. But when you bring intention and personal simplicity back to your rituals, self-care does indeed become a revolutionary act. It gives you the energy to fight, to figure things out, to take care of your immediate world and the one at large, to follow what energizes you, to quite literally illuminate the world—yours and others'—into a brighter place we all believe it can be.

There's one woman I look up to the most, for her life that's designed around rituals and self-care: Latham Thomas. She's a lifestyle maven, a doula to amazing women like Alicia Keys, and one of Oprah's SuperSoul 100 teachers. And she's a dear friend, someone who's taught me by example what it means to always return home to ourselves in order to find the right path forward.

"When you plug your phone into the wall and you use it, it never runs out of juice. But when you unplug it and you start using it and it's down to twenty percent, you start freaking out looking for an outlet." That's what happens to us every day, she explains. You have to keep coming back to what recharges you, or you end up in the red and you get all frazzled. "You're constantly thinking about how your phone stays charged, but are you asking yourself that?"

You have to come back to what gives you the most space and energy, especially when you're feeling worried and unclear about your future. Self-care is what allows you to understand if maybe that left turn should have been a right turn. It allows you to actually hear yourself instead of the million messages coming from anywhere but within.

"Self-care is a pathway to empowerment," Latham told me. Because as she sees it, it allows you to be more of who you already are, and it helps you return to that person when you need it, instead of trying to become who everyone else wants you to be. "When you have these moments sitting in a bathtub and massaging your skin, reading a good book, going for a hike, or going on a bike ride and feeling the air moving through your hair, you're not thinking about your thighs—you're thinking about the grace and the beauty of that moment and you're living it." And so you can build your confidence by becoming more in touch with and aware of what your intuition is telling you.

My personal favorite rituals for tapping into my own strong energy:

Eating lunch outside without my phone
Taking a nap with a heated lavender eye pillow
Getting in a morning sweat
Lying down in the shower
Putting on lipstick
Lighting a candle (you already know which one)
Going to sleep early

STEP AWAY FROM THE SCREEN

Let's take a hot second to talk about our phones. As you can see, most of the ways I tap back into my own energy have to do with things that aren't digital. While phones and computers and Wi-Fi allow me to do the work that I do, they also detract from the strength and positive energy needed for that work. Consider how tethered you actually are to your phone and the onslaught of information coming out of it.

Last month, I even went so far as calling my phone provider in total frustration to see if there were any options that would allow me to keep my plan while also having a less high-tech phone—preferably one that only sent and accepted calls and texts. Craig, my lovely customer service representative, listened intently as I rambled through questions:

"Is there any way to have an iPhone when I want it, but maybe to switch my SIM card to a dumb phone when I want that instead? Or is there any way to have both a smartphone and a dumb phone with the same number and plan?" I pleaded.

Not understanding my problem, Craig responded, "Ma'am, I'm not sure I understand the point of these questions. Is your goal here to save money?"

To which I responded, "No, Craig, my goal here is to save my soul."

Which was true. I'd spent too many consecutive hours on my phone and I literally wanted to throw it out the freaking window. I dreamt of going off the grid into no-woman's land, where no one could like my photos, no one could email me, and I didn't have to respond to a single text message or email ever again.

The amount of time that I spent on my phone was coming to a head. Did you know that you're using your phone twice as many times in a day as you think you are—for an average of five hours a day?[1] (I can say I likely use mine way more than that.) We are in an information overload from messages and voices that aren't our own. In the same way we're in the habit of coming back to our phones first thing in the morning, we have to learn rituals that allow us to step away from the digital world to see and feel and hear our true selves.

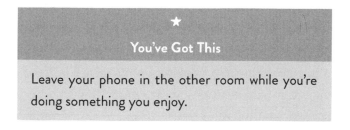

★

You've Got This

Leave your phone in the other room while you're doing something you enjoy.

Rituals that leave digital devices behind are a form of self-care, and they can also become a renewable energy source for summoning the strength you need to act. And these actions are the same ones that breed confidence. Putting yourself first is integral in pushing off all those feelings of doubt, confusion, and lack. You can combat anxiety by returning to your true strength. And rituals can take you on that return flight, every time.

RATIONAL ILLOGIC

Sometimes people who rely on rituals can be perceived as total quacks. Because when a baseball player has to tap his left shoulder three times and kiss the cross on his necklace before he goes up to bat, it's unclear whether it's just a ritual or he has some baseline compulsion.

Regardless of how off the rocker some rituals may seem, some of the most successful people around use them to their advantage. We see interesting superstitious acts in all types of people. It's said that Taylor Swift swears by the number 13; Barack Obama carries a tiny idol of Hanuman with him; Justin Bieber does push-ups before his show; Michael Jordan wore the same pair of blue North Carolina shorts under his NBA uniform for most of his career; and Serena Williams bounces every tennis ball five times before serving.

All these commitments to repetitive meaningful acts performed before major, high-stakes situations are in fact found to reduce anxiety and increase confidence in the people performing them. And, get this, even people who say they don't believe in rituals benefit.

There have been all kinds of studies about rituals like hearing "I'll cross my fingers for you" or receiving a "lucky" golf ball before performing a golf swing, and they all reveal the same results: Our confidence in our ability to succeed is heightened, our effort is motivated, and our performance improves when we do these rituals (or someone does them for us) before we execute something important.[2]

Completing rituals with the *intention* to do something well actually translates to a better performance.[3] Positive performances are key in taking bigger and bigger steps forward—so why not try your hand at a lucky charm or ritualized superstition? You can borrow them from other people or figure out one for yourself.

When I was first beginning my speaking career and obviously insanely nervous that I'd bomb the stages that people paid me to be on, I read something on social media about how one of my favorite authors and speakers never went onstage without her mala (a string of beads traditionally used in prayer and meditation). At the time, I happened to be in a country that harvested rudraksha, which are seeds that traditional Hindu malas are made of, and I decided I needed to find out what these are all about.

I found a woman about an hour away with a rudraksha workshop, met with her, and learned that her entire life's mission was to bring the power of these beads to the West in the right way. I went from never having heard of any of this to wearing the beads nonstop, to this day. Every stage, every video, every writing day, knowing these beads are there makes me feel a little more in my groove—my borrowed lucky charm.

Whether you have lucky charms already (hello, lucky underpants!) or a promising ritual (Oprah candle, anyone?), try asking other people what works for them. And then think about what works for you. What makes you feel unstoppable? What makes you feel supported? What makes you feel grounded? What makes you feel courageous? Do that. And do that, every time—every single time—you go to take on what you'd consider an important opportunity. Whether it's a client call, an interview, public speaking, hitting PUBLISH, or sending a cold-call email. Your lucky charm is the perfect Wite-Out for the Sharpie of doubt.

Your potential is there. Your ability to take bigger and bigger steps in your path is undeniable. You can *literally* do absolutely anything that you have the capacity to dream about. But in the days and weeks leading up to that curtain rising, know that you've gone into it without being out on a limb, but instead being cradled by the rituals you've created to support your success. *That* is just another tool in your box of self-belief, so that when the curtain falls you know you'll have your own personal standing ovation.

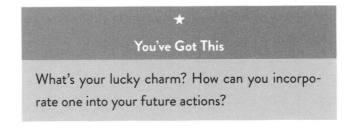

★

You've Got This

What's your lucky charm? How can you incorporate one into your future actions?

FEEL YOUR WAY FORWARD

Images are a powerful, powerful thing. And most of us have grown up with an insane amount of visual storytelling everywhere we look. From computers to phone screens to TVs to our camera rolls, we know how to capture and understand both imaginary stories and past ones using visuals. But the real power of images is that they help us connect emotionally.

Now, I'm about to mention a self-help trope that I want you to *not* roll your eyes at: visualizing success. This is a strategy that when done wrong just becomes 2005 bullshit that gets misunderstood, misconstrued, and used the wrong way. If you've ever lain on the couch and imagined yourself feeling all the feels of winning an award, of finding out you got that big job, or any other endgame success, basically you've gotten the strategy of visualization all wrong.

Visualizing the *process* of success, rather than its outcome, is the real power behind this technique. What most of us do, however, is visualize the outputs of success, which is proven to be completely ineffective. Not only does visualizing the end goal zap our energy, but creating positive fantasies about the future results in less motivation to go after the end goal that we're visualizing.[4] I know, I know, it's not everything you read on the internet.

What *is* shown to work is getting down to the nitty-gritty of the process leading to your successful outcome.

Think about it: Professional athletes who are famously known to visualize their success before every game or match don't see themselves standing in front of the crowd holding the big trophy. No.

What they're visualizing are things that they control. What they're spending their energy and time emotionally connecting to is their shot, their form, their composure—all of which they have full agency over.

So you can turn visualizing the process into a powerful ritual for seeing your ability to achieve the outcome you desire. And here's the deal: In order to get to the future you want to be in, you'll be required to do some things. When it comes to that doing, no matter what it is, no matter how mundane, no matter how small, if you think it's an important step, then using the tool of visualizing the process will help. Getting into the details of your path, like all the details, is the way you can actually make visualization work for you.

See yourself having that tough conversation and speaking calmly.

See yourself making the cold phone call to ask for a meeting with ease.

See yourself sitting down to something creative and feeling total joy in it.

Visualize your desired process for doing it, instead of the outcome that you want. Whatever step you need to take, visualize your desired process for doing it, instead of the outcome that you want. Try to see yourself in the middle of all the details of the task—not after it, not celebrating it, not being lauded for it. No, see yourself in the thick of a future step and navigating it beautifully no matter the hardship, the doubt, or the rain of confusion you feel.

★
You've Got This

Close your eyes. Imagine a goal. Now see yourself going through the process of getting there.

Rituals, whether visualization or any other repetitive positive behavior, are a practice. They're habits that take time to form. But when we can see and feel the benefits of doing something consistently, the ritual easily becomes something we turn to instead of being just another *should* on that long list of to-dos.

Obviously, the *how* is the hard part. Or perhaps, the *how to commit*. It's something we're all trying to figure out. Consider New Year's resolutions and our cultural obsession with them, for example. Most times, we choose goals and habits we want to commit to. But unfortunately, most of these resolutions fail miserably. This occurs because we create resolutions to tackle big things we "should" do, rather than committing to small and meaningful practices that are deeply rooted in a desire bigger than any arbitrary goal.

Small changes made in the name of taking care of yourself, ones that are based on keeping open a highway of clarity to your truest self, are far more powerful than ones created because you *think you should*. Intention is what separates us from *should*ing all over ourselves and instead putting powerful rituals into practice. Take meditation, for example. Everyone talks about how important and healthy it is, but if you sit down for an hour to meditate because it's what you're "supposed" to do, you'll likely fail. What you'll miss is the benefit of trying it for, say, five minutes—because that's the calm and quiet your mind actually needed.

In the research around committing to new habits—in our case, rituals or practices of self-care—there's an idea called "keystone habits," coined by Charles Duhigg in *The Power of Habit*.[5] Like in architecture, in which the keystone is the crucial last piece that locks all the other stones into place and bears the weight of an arch, a keystone habit is that one thing we do consistently that we can build other desired habits around. It's encouragement, in my mind, to start in one place—with one change that can help us feel closer and more intimate with our own intuition and energy—and then build upon that. This isn't a call to change everything at once, but to make one change that positively impacts everything.

My keystone habit started with a practice of being **batshit grateful—the ritual to end all rituals**.

Listen, like you I'm often thinking about where the future will go and how I can squeeze as much out of it as possible.

If you think no one questions whether they're doing enough or going far enough or whether they're a little bit lost, you're not talking to enough people. All of us, myself included, have intense moments of wondering, of wandering.

And there will always be more to strive toward. There will always be more that others seem to be achieving. There will always be a dangling golden carrot in the future. And unless you get rooted in where you're at and find joy and appreciation in that, you're destined to stay in a permanent state of confusion.

Over the course of my introduction to the self-help world, I had probably started and attempted to stick to a gratitude ritual about a million times. It was actually closer to six—always a part of my New Year's resolutions, or every time an article hit me on Facebook about why gratitude would make my life better. For whatever reason, I just couldn't get it to stick. I even created a devoted email account in what was almost my final attempt to chronicle my appreciation daily. I figured I sent about a hundred emails a day; surely I could find time for one that included the three things I'm most grateful for.

But damn if I just wouldn't stick to it. Until (I should probably just rename this chapter after her) I was reading Oprah's *What I Know for Sure*. In it she recounts a story, from the height of her success, when she was feeling the most unfulfilled. When she examined why that was, she realized that while journaling her gratitude had always been a ritual she'd kept up with, she'd stopped as her show got bigger and bigger. And here she was with everything any human could ever want and she wasn't feeling it.

In that moment, in that story, because of Oprah's story of success and the lack of corresponding feelings to go along with it, I picked my nightly gratitude journaling back up. Three things every night in my small white moleskine.

When you consistently come back to a place of being batshit grateful (as I like to call it), you're literally training your brain to feel all the amazing feels of *enough*. It helps to chill out about the big picture that you can't control and settle into a trust and appreciation for what exists all around you right now. Gratitude has been proven time and time again to promote feelings of well-being.[6] Gratitude is helpful when things are good, and maybe even more important when things are really tough, when they don't go the right way or you're facing a frustrating rough patch of progress. At both ends of the spectrum, a gratitude ritual can keep you from wishing away your life.

There are plenty of ways to make gratitude part of your daily life. I think my failed email strategy was a smart one for the right person. Journaling is an old faithful. Telling one person every day that you're grateful for them and why works too. You can also just close your eyes and quietly review all that you appreciate from your day. There's not a right or a wrong way, unless you're ignoring this one ritual that will always bring you back to the present goodness of your life.

AN ENVIRONMENT TO THRIVE

Like plants in need of the right light and moisture, you're going to need the right combination of energies in order to stay tuned in to just how powerful you are, as you are. Tapping into that requires pushing away the external and coming back into the internal. Your rituals will always be a way to come back to it. Confidence isn't something you have to wait to feel. It's something you should be ritualizing as a part of your daily experience.

When you're nervous, rituals will calm. When you're questioning, they'll answer. When you're freaked out, they'll chill you out. When you're tired, they'll energize you. When you're flighty, they'll anchor you. Practicing rituals will reinstate the balance you need, when you need it, to get after what's next and feel good about it. They don't have to be daily practices; they don't even have to be weekly.

The question, then, is what do *you* need? What do you need every day? What energy do you require the most right now to believe that you can clear the fog you might be feeling and return to your most powerful self, the version of yourself who doesn't doubt the steps she's taking (or needs to take) to follow her truth?

WORKSHEET
Feel It

What type of energy do you currently feel that you'd like to let go of?

Is there anything in your day-to-day that triggers this feeling the most?

Can you think of one thing you can do to change that pattern so it's not in your day-to-day as much?

What type of energy do you want to feel in the coming weeks in order to take your small steps forward?

Is there anything simple that makes you feel that way day-to-day?

Try outlining your week to find something each day that gives you the energy you need. Write some ideas in the boxes.

	Sunday	Monday	Tuesday	Wednesday	Thursday	Friday	Saturday
read							
eat							
move/do							
meditate							
gratitude							
connect							
other							

Calendar it. Schedule a recurring reminder into your calendar to do these simple things that give you the "I can do this" energy you need.

CHAPTER 7

Acting As If

*Just believe in yourself. Even if you don't, pretend
that you do and, at some point, you will.*
—VENUS WILLIAMS

WHEN FIGURING SOMETHING OUT or doing something new, we assume that we need the exact plan and knowledge in order to execute. We think that through perfect understanding and know-how we will see a pathway to greatness. We expect to know exactly what we're doing before we do it—because isn't that how it works? Well, maybe in school.

In real life, almost nothing works that way, including paving a powerful path forward. Yes, Malcolm Gladwell with his 10,000 Hour Rule shows that practice will make you one of the greats. It's not, however, needed in order to start. And it is definitely not needed in order to do well once you begin.

When you look around at all the people taking risks, creating things, and fully marching forward on their paths, our giant-ass misconception is that these people know exactly what they're doing.

We brainwash ourselves into believing that successful and confident people don't also doubt themselves immensely. Basically, we make up an entire story in our heads about how those other people had it all figured out before they started.

I know how it goes. You have a little seed of a future dream that's planted itself inside you. It's that little kick of energy. It's that nugget of inspiration. And you're feeling the momentum of excitement. Until *bam!* You see someone doing what you wanted to do, but they're doing it *so* well. And they're *so* successful. And they're doing it with so much grace and confidence that you feel as if one of Harry Potter's Dementors has come by and literally sucked the soul right out of you, taking the exciting idea you had right along with it.

I can't compete with that.

They're so sure of themselves and what they're doing.

I don't know how to actually do this.

Herein lies your problem. During this crazed comparison to someone from the internet who you've likely never met (and thus have no idea what's actually going on inside their head), you forget an important truth: No one knows what they're doing most of the time. We're all just winging it. But they started anyway. And those who tend to figure out their paths and continue to grow and accomplish are the ones who don't let doubt stop them. They're willing to doubt themselves and act anyway. They're willing to move forward despite feeling like they're just making it up as they go along. Acting in the face of doubt *is* how you go about believing in yourself and believing that you can.

> No one knows what they're doing most of the time. We're all just winging it.

BREAKING THROUGH

Most career turning points happen when you step into a willingness to wing it. Let me clarify winging it: I don't mean that you don't practice, study, rehearse, or put in some real preparation or effort. However, none of that will help you feel like you've done this before if you haven't. Winging it is about never having done it before and doing it anyway. The amount of times I've *acted* like I knew what I was doing even though I really didn't directly correlates to every time I've stepped into an exciting new level of my career. Because in order for us to expand, we have to step into uncertainty.

Now, let's clear one thing up: This isn't about *lying* about your skills on a résumé or covering up your inexperience in an interview. This isn't about *faking it until you make it*, because PSA, I hate that phrase—we're not faking anything. We're stepping into our truest selves; ain't nothing fake about that. This is simply about creating your future by trying and doing what excites you regardless of your doubts and despite the fact that you've never done it before.

We all have career turning points. And when I define mine, I see that right alongside them were immense feelings of *But I have no idea what I'm doing*.

Reading off a teleprompter: Hadn't done it until I was on a set of the NFL Network filming demo clips for my reel. I figured if I could read, I'd be fine. I was awful. But I was fine.

Building out a global community network: Hadn't done it. But I wrote out a local community plan that got me the job. Before I knew it I was managing thirty cities and forty-plus volunteer leaders and being mentored by the best community experts in the space. I'd never done any of that before. But it changed my entire life.

Negotiating talent contracts: Hadn't done it. Until someone asked me for my contract. So I went to Google, naturally. Threw my logo on it. Got the deal and got paid.

Running my own business: Hadn't done it. But I figured a good business coach could teach me what I would only find out the hard way otherwise, so I hired one.

Emceeing a major conference: Never been there, never done that. Until there were four hundred people staring at me onstage with a mic in my hand as I kicked off the day. And it became my new favorite thing.

Funding a video series: Hadn't done it until I made up a pitch deck with my producing partner, shopped it out, and found myself on the phone pitching a VP of AOL. I butchered that call and it didn't go anywhere. But I sure as hell learned.

Going on a press tour: Hadn't done it. Until I was the spokesperson for a Fortune 50 company's campaign and had a full day of interviews with everyone under the sun, including *Seventeen*, *Women's Health*, Refinery29, and *Marie Claire*. I nailed those press interviews and had more media coverage in a week than I'd had in my whole career combined.

Writing a book proposal: Hadn't done it. So I googled other people's proposals and then I bought a ninety-nine-dollar guide to help me out. I asked a bunch of talented writers I knew to review it. And before I knew it, the proposal I didn't know how to write was written and agents were reviewing (and rejecting) it.

These were all pretty major moments in my hunt for direction. Each of them was a little turning point. Had I not gone for it, I wouldn't be here.

Did I feel doubt in each of these situations? Oh you can bet your bottom dollar on it. I can vividly remember before that press tour, which included my first major *live* network TV interview—I was up all night in my hotel room curled around a trash can. My stomach was in the worst knots and my anxiety was manifesting itself in full-on nausea as I thought about all the potential ways I could screw up this thing that I'd technically never done before.

But I refused to let the nerves of *I've never done this* stop me. I woke up that morning, painted on my TV network game face, and showed up to the interview. As I sat just off set with the team running this press tour, I pointed up to a call board that had my name next to a "Money Matters" segment. *WTF?* I thought. *I'm not here to talk about money; I'm here to talk about landing your dream job.* I tried not to have a mini–panic attack about some error being made and the idea of adjusting on the fly to present the content I had prepared through a money lens. We tried to get ahold of the executive producer to double-check, but with no success. Before I knew it, I was sitting on set with a camera pointed directly at my face in a tight shot, lights everywhere. Seconds before going live I had no clue if the host was about to ask me money questions or ask me about what I was there to talk about, but I was ready and willing to wing whatever came my way. These things happen, I told myself, and you've got to believe that all of your hard work and prep will help you navigate whatever clusterfuck might be ahead in this situation.

There was a split second between when the host started talking and when I could process what he was saying. Time felt like it was suspended. As soon as I realized his first question was laying out everything I had intended to talk about, time sped back up and I calmed down. I was thrown an almost-curveball and I knocked it out of the damn park, which is why I can't look at that clip without smiling. Somehow doing a great job is always made better by the nerves and trepidation and bumps that precede it. It's a reminder that we're goddamn princess warriors.

I'm in a constant state of winging it, as are many people I look up to, and the same probably goes for many of the people you look up to. You can do things you've never done before; you can adjust to things that don't go according to plan and still crush it. Expanding into a path that you're excited about will demand it. And the more of these situations you get through, the more confident you'll become. You'll be able to think back and say, *I survived that. I will survive this.*

DISCOMFORT IS IMPERATIVE

Contrary to this *Come on, girl, be willing to wing it!* advice—and this is going to come as a disappointment (most likely)—you're not actually going to stop worrying the next time you do something new. You'll still feel wildly uncomfortable. You'll likely still doubt, and fret, and worry just a bit. BUT the edge will soften a bit because you'll know . . . like really know, that this is what you're supposed to be feeling and it's what everyone else is feeling too.

That awareness, often, is the solution. It's not FEWER uncomfortable feelings that we should expect. It's simply knowing, identifying, and being aware of those feelings, seeing them for what they are, and going headfirst into action anyways.

Discomfort is imperative to pushing your path forward. *IMPERATIVE.* If you're not feeling it, you're not doing shit. Point blank. You can look at how uncomfortable you feel as a direct meter read of how much you're expanding in your life. Or as a mentor once told me, "If you're in your comfort zone, you're probably not taking over the world."

You want life to be getting bigger, right? Well, as it does—as *you* do—that expansion comes with feelings and discomfort that are bigger too. Your doubts will still be there to make you question your abilities and second-guess your decisions. It's about learning to push past those doubts.

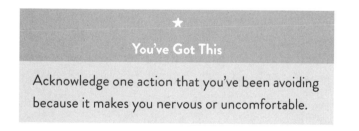

★

You've Got This

Acknowledge one action that you've been avoiding because it makes you nervous or uncomfortable.

I have to remind myself of this all the time. *All* the time. And I often joke with people that for all the major moments in my life that catapulted me into further clarity on my path, I've wanted to avoid them *so* badly. Because every time, the big thing I needed to do felt so wildly uncomfortable.

I've never wanted to bail on something more, however, than at an event that should have been plucked right out of my wildest dreams: speaking at a massive women's leadership conference in NYC and hosting the live broadcast that allowed everyone who wasn't there to watch from home. It was *everything* I'd said I wanted to be doing, everything I wanted to be moving toward. I was given a *big-time* stage to do just that.

And what was I doing the morning of the conference? Hiding in the bathroom, stuffing tissues into my armpits to soak up the sweat from my full-on freak-out, and dreaming up seven hundred different ways I could bail. Expanding like I was that day, into my vision for the future, I was feeling everything we normally feel in this situation. And I could see the freak-out for what it was: not a sign to *actually* bail, but a sign that I was expanding.

And thank God I didn't bail. Hosting that Livestream broadcast was a turning point for me in *knowing* that I wanted to be back on camera and remembering that I had a talent for it. Those sports broadcasting days weren't for nothing. And speaking in front of five hundred people—the biggest crowd I'd ever been in front of up to the time—after they'd just seen the business queen that is Diane von Furstenberg give her keynote interview, was a launching pad for my entire speaking career. I still recall that memory whenever I'm nervous and unsure of myself, and I think, *If I could handle that, I can handle the thing in front of me.* The times when you want to bail the most are likely the learning moments you need the most.

And so expansion goes. Think about the stretch marks women get as their bellies expand from pregnancy or their thighs expand during puberty—growing comes with real pains and signs of change. But what's actually happening is that you are being asked to meet the size of your dreams.

Smallness feels more comfortable. Bigness looks more comfortable. But in between those two stages is the demand to expand. Realize what's going on and always push your path to a place that feels uncomfortable—and don't shy away from it. You'll like where it's leading you if you just keep going.

A SIGN OF GREATNESS

It's possible to second-guess yourself right out of an amazing opportunity. Because when you're on the sidelines watching people in the game and on fire, it can be intimidating. When you get thrown in, it's easy to wonder: *Should I be here? Do I deserve to be playing?*

Maybe someone will find out that I have no idea what I'm doing.

Oh, impostor syndrome. It's the feeling that you'll be exposed as a fraud for not knowing what you're doing or feeling, as if you're not experienced enough to be where you're at. Comically, I once heard Ann Shoket, former editor in chief of *Seventeen*, say it's a term she can't stand, because it sounds like as a society we've clinically diagnosed anyone who doubts themselves (which is all of us at some point, somewhere). I couldn't agree with her more. This isn't some life-inhibiting condition. In fact, it's actually the sign of a high achiever. And most people I know have felt this way at some point.

Even *the* Maya Angelou (Nobel laureate, activist, and poet) famously shared, "I have written eleven books, but each time I think, 'uh-oh, they're going to find out now. I've run a game on everybody, and they're going to find me out.'"[1] She's not alone. Amy Schumer, Jessica Chastain, and Sheryl Sandberg have all said they've experienced feelings of being a fraud and doubting their own success.[2]

I most *definitely* felt that way when I took that stage in NYC. It wasn't just that it was a big moment for me, it was also that so many of the women in the room had *decades* of experience on me, yet they were all there to learn from what I had to say. I thought incessantly about how there was no way they'd take me seriously, that maybe there was no way I could even provide value to them, that I legitimately didn't deserve to be there talking to these women who were looking for real inspiration and actions to take for their lives and businesses. Someone had definitely made a mistake.

But the line that formed after my workshop session proved the total opposite. These women from all ages and walks of life thanked me, complimented me, hugged me, and reaffirmed my right to be there. I was so happy I hadn't followed my impulse to bail.

Do not pass up opportunities because you doubt that you have what it takes. You must say yes. You must get off the sidelines. You deserve to be there and to be here.

HOW TO ACTUALLY DEAL

The gap between feeling your doubt and taking action anyway can be treacherous if you give doubt the limelight, because knowing your doubt is there and dealing with it are two very different things. Sometimes you've got to talk yourself off the bathroom toilet hideout where you're about three steps from bailing and get your butt onto the stage, whether that critical voice is there or not. And then go act like you own the place.

Have you ever been at a restaurant where some strange face who is *not* the waiter comes up to your table and asks you how your night is going, if you're liking the food, if you're enjoying yourself, if there's anything else you need? While you have no clue who this person is, you don't doubt the conversation for a second. They're comfortable, they're owning it, and thus they must *literally* own the place.

It is the owner, obviously. You know it almost instantly. And if it's not the owner it's the general manager or someone else in charge. They walk around like they own the place, and so you don't think twice about a stranger coming up to your table, interrupting your meal, and talking to you. They're confident, so you're confident in them.

In the situations you fear the most, taking the attitude of the owner is one that will not only calm you but also instill confidence in those listening to you, working with you, partnering with you, sitting in your meeting, and investing in you. Whatever the opportunity is, whatever the discomfort is, act like you deserve to be there and not only will you start to believe it—everyone else will too.

Much of why this works has to do with our body's ability to affect our confidence rather than the other way around. We're so used to letting our feelings predict our actions, but actually we can minimize our doubt, fear, and hesitancy by letting our actions lead us to confidence. It's known as the principle of *act as if*.[3]

It's been proven time and time again: Hold your fist clenched and you have more willpower. Sit on a hard chair and you negotiate

better. Act like you're in love with the person next to you and you feel
in love. We have more power over our emotions and feelings than we
give ourselves credit for.

If you behave as if you're a certain type of person, you'll become
that person. This is based on decades of research that proves that in a
wide variety of situations, if you act a certain way, you'll actually begin feeling and believing that very thing. Act like you're confident
and you will feel confident.

When you're feeling like there's a delta between how you feel and
how you want to be perceived, *act as if*. And sometimes it's helpful on
hard days to channel the person you'd like to be, to act as if you're
them.

After seeing Wonder Woman played by Gal Gadot, my girlfriends
and I were next-level inspired—I was crying when it started and crying when it ended. We spent the following seventy-two hours texting
each other about our Wonder Woman Halloween costume plans and
sorting out ways we could use connections to have them 3-D printed.
The inspiration culminated in this text from the girls: "Now in every
decision I make, I ask myself: What Would Wonder Woman
Do/Say?"

WWWWD. It was done. I decided that my *act as if* mindset
would be channeled via Wonder Woman from now on. Just the idea
of her standing up for what was right, not taking no for an answer,
not letting anyone shut her up or tell her otherwise helped me so
much. She immediately became the person who in situations where I
doubted myself, I wanted to act as if . . . as if I was Wonder Woman.
Would Wonder Woman worry about the tone of the email she just
received? No. Would Wonder Woman hold her tongue about this?

No. Would Wonder Woman feel out of place speaking to this group? Nope. She'd let nothing stop her from accomplishing what she believed in, and she'd let nothing stop her from believing in herself and acting on that confidence.

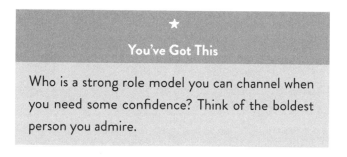

★

You've Got This

Who is a strong role model you can channel when you need some confidence? Think of the boldest person you admire.

SHADOWING MASTERY

Acting as if becomes a far easier prescription for success when you have a clear idea of what the hell that actually looks like in practice. There's a reason role models and success stories are such powerful tools for inspiration, allowing us to believe that we can get where we want to be one day—because they allow you to see through the doubt.

If you don't know what confidently acting out your future actually looks like, there's one really spectacular way to go about finding out. Watch the masters of your desired future. And watch them closely. The majority of things that we learn come from mirroring other people.

Do I believe education is important? Of course. Is continued learning imperative? Absolutely. And while there are about a million resources to help us all do this, there's also under-championed, old-school apprenticeship that we often ignore when thinking about stepping into our best selves.

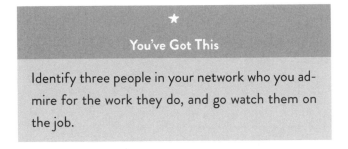

★

You've Got This

Identify three people in your network who you admire for the work they do, and go watch them on the job.

The purpose of watching people isn't to do *exactly* what they do. It's to pick up on what it looks like to do some of your dreams well. And to witness how they act confidently when you might be doubting yourself.

There are a few people I watch like a hawk:

Brené Brown. I observe her openness, her presence, and how she's created education and books that light your soul on fire.

Oprah. Obvi. I watch videos and speeches of her about once a month to study how she interviews, how she tells stories, how she listens, and how she communicates.

Tiffany Dufu. She was one of the first mentors on my journey who I got to shadow in real life. I'm always paying attention to how she inspires anyone who interacts with her.

Danielle LaPorte. For her writing, her spirituality, and how she's created a digital empire of good.

I will never be Brené, Oprah, Tiffany, or Danielle. And I don't want to be. I do, however, immensely admire their work and how they do it. I've put so many lessons into practice because of things I saw them do, in real life and from afar, to see how those lessons feel for me. I try their strategies on.

In your head you can want to do something, but when you actually get there, you have to remind yourself that you will always feel a resistance to believing that you can or that you're ready. However, when you've watched something done, and you've had time to see it in greatness mode, you'll be ready even if the action feels tough. You've already been shadowing exactly how it can look at its best. Step by step, you'll get to that point too. Not on the first try. But through lots of repetition of these things that energize you.

And it's always worth remembering that the people we look up to feel how we do, or felt how we do. But they did it anyway. Which is why they are where they are. In my opinion, Piera Gelardi, cofounder and executive creative director of Refinery29 (the mighty women's digital media and entertainment company), personifies acting in the face of her own doubt. I know this because of how openly and publicly she talks about the feelings that come along with her leadership and the critical voice inside her head. I'll never forget the first time I heard her speak. I had this overwhelming feeling of calm because I thought, *If* she *feels that, then it's OK that I'm feeling that way too.*

"My inner voice is very ambitious and a perfectionist. It has very high standards and never thinks anything is a home run," she told me. "It likes to go to a place of feeling like I don't know what I'm doing. It says I don't have the experience to be doing what I'm doing—that I didn't go to school for this. I didn't have a mentor that taught me how to do this. I didn't have a job that taught me how to do this. I don't know what I'm doing."

Sound familiar? Piera is all of us. So I had to know how she quiets that voice and creates all the magic at Refinery29 that she does.

"I push past it just by acknowledging my patterns. You'll realize that there are certain things that trigger those thoughts and there are certain thought patterns that you just default to. . . . I often default to feeling lost and like I don't know what I'm doing," she explained.

Piera outlined her strategies for dealing with that *I have no idea what I'm doing* feeling. First, she recognizes that she has self-doubting thoughts and that she has them often. She tries to pay attention to what triggers these things in her mind. Knowing the pattern won't stop them, she says, but it'll at least provide insight into what's going on.

Second, she has a document called "Feel Good Notes" where she puts any nice notes or comments that people send her about whatever she's done well—creative projects, leadership, mentoring, and so on. And she makes herself look at it, oftentimes begrudgingly and with great disbelief, whenever she's doubting herself. When she looks at these notes, there is a burden of proof that disputes everything going on in her head, and it becomes greater than the self-doubt, she says. Strategies like this are especially important when you're trying new things.

"They call them growing pains because they're a real thing. . . . It's a cliché at this point, but I think it's true that your comfort zone is your enemy in a lot of ways. **In order to grow, you need to go to uncomfortable places and you need to push through**," Piera says.

Leading a global media and entertainment company like Refinery29 has obviously been full of growing pains. So I wanted to know when Piera felt them the most. "There was a point where I was really comfortable as a creative director . . . but my role as cofounder also meant being an executive, a role that felt so foreign to me. At the time, I wondered if I needed to hire above myself, if someone else should lead in my place. Thinking it over, I realized *that's absurd*."

Often, the solutions that your brain creates for your doubt *are* totally absurd because they're solutions that hold you back and keep you small. Piera explains how to deal: "When I think about the option to turn opportunities down, I'm reminded what they always say about people and regrets—you regret more the things that you didn't do than the things that you *do*. I don't want to limit myself because something is hard or scary or uncomfortable. I want to at least give it a try."

A million times yes—you have to try. And keep trying. And not let your own doubt or uncertainty keep you from acting. Because we're all just winging it.

We're all just winging it.

WORKSHEET
Handle It

List all the times you did something important for the first time, but were scared shitless or doubted yourself before you did:

Now, which of those are you so happy you did? Rewrite them here:

Anytime you get scared to take a step forward, think about these moments. If you can handle those, you will handle whatever is ahead.

Create your own Feel Good Notes folder to look at whenever that doubty voice that says you don't know what you're doing rears its ugly head.

Rise

CHAPTER 8

A Small *P*

I long to accomplish a great and noble task, but it is
my chief duty to accomplish small tasks
as if they were great and noble.
—HELEN KELLER

WHAT IF I GAVE YOU a mandate to think small? Like, really tiny. Eensy-weensy. Small, small, small. I know it's counterintuitive. I know that big-picture thinking gets all the glory. But grand goals and master plans can cause major frustration. They become reminders of everywhere we're not already at.

You eat an elephant one bite at a time, so they say. And so too with anything that you're trying to figure out—one step at a time. So, you have to learn how to fall madly in love with small plans and even smaller steps. Because that's how you tap into the most confidently expressed version of yourself.

Starting always begins with something small. But somewhere we deemed small not good enough. Because if we're not there, then we don't want to be here. And, well, that's a recipe for going nowhere.

Everything you eventually do in your life happens because of tiny moments. But for some reason, when it comes to creating your future, tiny is no longer acceptable. Think about what it takes to go on a dreamy vacation and how you get to the point of experiencing it. You made a chronological and meaningful series of small choices in order to be lying on the beach. You researched a location. You booked a flight. You confirmed accommodations. You checked the weather. You packed a bag. You got yourself to the airport. You boarded a plane. You showed up. This small plans thing . . . you *know* how to do this. You do this every day in myriad ways; you just need to start doing it with the unknown that is your future direction.

Building a deep sense of belief in your path and allowing future goals to unfold both require that you show up for yourself every day. You must let your small steps mean something. You must allow day-by-day plans to feel as worthy as the grand ones.

Reconnecting with the value of little wins will bring your power back. How do you think many of the most successful Team USA swimmers train for the biggest competition of their lives? They train to reach competency and satisfaction in minor achievements, which in turn gives them more confidence to go after even more small wins each and every day.[1] These small wins build on each other until the one win that really matters: the Olympics.

Olympians are using this strategy to confidently create a possible future that holds the biggest accolade of their lives. Why should we be any different in creating our future dreams?

You only get *there* by starting *here*. Let your choices be good enough. Let the small steps be worthy in your eyes.

The deal with small plans, though, is not only that we don't deem them worthy enough, it's also that we don't want to sit in our discomfort without the glory. We want the immediate satisfaction that this thing we're doing is definitely going to get us where we want to go. This hell of a day, or of a plan, is going to be the thing that lands us there.

You've got to drop your obsession with recognition like it's hot. And *trust* yourself, that you'll get that glory eventually, that you'll get to where you want to be. You have to allow today to count. Today is what matters most of all, even if it is nondescript, boring, and mundane. You've got to commit to the going when the going is boring as fuck.

> **You've got to commit to the going when the going is boring as fuck.**

If I had looked for big plans and even bigger excitement in order to justify my dreams, I would have stopped going after them all those years ago. Because those first years (and lots of days even still) can be so unrewarding day-to-day, because the steps are tiny. My everyday is anything but glamorous. And the small plans it took to get here, to today, were just as unglamorous.

Teaching myself WordPress and MailChimp and Photoshop using YouTube tutorials on Sundays . . . *not glam.*

Writing blog posts twice a week that no one read besides, like, ten people and my family . . . *not glam.*

Reviewing, editing, and tweaking website wireframes week after week for six months . . . *not glam.*

Writing corporate blog posts for a little extra income . . . *not glam.*

Running around San Francisco like a crazy person trying to get all the right props for a photo shoot . . . *not glam.*

Spending my weekends building out workshops while other people were brunching . . . *not glam.*

Re-creating my media kit for hours and hours because the people originally in charge of it couldn't get it right . . . *not glam.*

Pitching speaking agents who never return phone calls or emails, or when they do, send rejections . . . *not glam.*

Negotiating contracts with prickly personalities back and forth for days . . . *not glam.*

But I do the not-glam stuff, daily, because I trust that these small plans are laddering into something bigger than me. So I just keep making them, because every time I find my way through some small feat that I had doubted myself in (like all of the above), I get more excited that I'll be able to take on bigger, more meaningful challenges ahead.

It's honoring the small plans—making them, creating them, and doing them—that led me to my big moments, my Olympics, like giant conferences that I keynoted, or filming a national TV segment. Because of so many of those small moments, I trust I can do a slammin' job on the really big ones. And I do. But it was because of the small plans repeated over and over that I even had the chance to get there to begin with.

If you're suffocating with how many small plans are between here and there and how much there is to do to get somewhere other than where you are, you're not alone. Sometimes it's the biggest thing that stops us from doing anything small right now. Because there are *too many* small things. There's *too much* to do. So I'll ask you the one question I'm always asking myself: What is the absolute smallest thing you can do right now to get closer to where you want to be?

> **What is the absolute smallest thing you can do right now to get closer to where you want to be?**

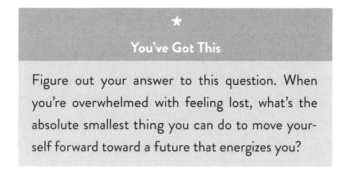

★

You've Got This

Figure out your answer to this question. When you're overwhelmed with feeling lost, what's the absolute smallest thing you can do to move yourself forward toward a future that energizes you?

In the many moments I've asked myself this question, it's been the smallest plans that have made the biggest impact. Research writing classes. Read that book about the topic. Send that one email asking for an introduction. Buy the domain name. These plans are boring and unmemorable, but they're the stepping-stones to the big stuff.

LITTLE PLANS, BIG FEEDBACK

When we feel lost, we obsess over the big plan that we're sure will get us out of our fog. It's all-consuming and completely unhelpful. Little plans, on the other hand, will give you time to make small, less risky efforts, which means something super important: You get small and meaningful feedback along the way. It's the difference between quitting your job only to find out that you hate the new industry you're in and doing a small side project in that industry and realizing you hate it before you lose your steady income. Small can very much be better, because it's a continuous feedback loop that can protect you from major meltdowns.

Consider charting a course in a boat. If you're off even a few tenths of a degree, after a hundred miles, you'll be so far off that getting back to your intended destination will be way harder than if you had made mile-by-mile plans to check in on your progress and see where you were at. You could have recalibrated. And that recalibration is exactly what small plans allow you to do.

When you start small, you get to start anywhere. That's the point, to take the pressure off being perfect and allow yourself to just begin. Starting small means you can keep moving forward and improve on where you began, or have something small to throw out completely if you want. You're most likely never going to love what you start with, but you will love what you build it into eventually. That's what we don't realize about most people's careers or projects or outcomes: They all started small and they started from wherever they were. But then they refined, and refined, and refined, and refined again to end up at this successful and exciting place that we see today.

But you can't refine, and you can't recalibrate, if you have no starting place. Starting small prevents you from wasting time. Because look, sometimes we get it wrong about what we want. Sometimes we contradict ourselves. Sometimes we need to start from scratch. That means you're growing, learning, and trying things. Allow yourself the space and knowledge to figure out whether a particular direction is indeed the one you want to continue to pursue, and don't be scared to change your mind. If you don't try it on and feel it out, you'll never know.

THE REAL COMMITMENT

Most people will tell you that to get your momentum, you need to commit to your dream, full stop. If you really want it, you'll hustle your little heart out. You won't let *anything* stop you. You'll do whatever it takes, they say.

But it's not your future, or your success, or your big plans, or even your small plans that need your commitment. It's not some future destination. It's none of that.

There's only one thing that needs your commitment in order for you to move forward, little step by little step. And that's you.

You need your commitment more than anything in the world. Small goals require it. When you commit to yourself, the small actions become easier. They become choices. They become excitement.

But sometimes committing to yourself is actually the hardest commitment you'll ever make. It demands that you believe you can do it, that you can stick with it, that you can bounce back from the hiccups that will happen.

It can be hard to see how the tiniest of actions are laddering you to where you want to be. Because while you're in them you don't always want to be doing them (duh). And when that happens, when you wake up to a laundry list of bullshit that you don't actually see the value in, you have to assess if there is something on that list for the day that is moving you forward to a future that energizes you. If the answer is yes, but you still feel unmotivated . . . you still feel less than excited . . . you still feel like there's no point, come back to your commitment to yourself by thinking not about the you of today, but the you of next year.

Science has shown that you're not a bad person because you prioritize the wrong things or because you chase instant gratification each day. It's actually quite normal to operate around what gives you satisfaction now rather than later.[2] However, while we all do this, it's also the same immediate trade-off that keeps us from achieving long-term, desired results.

Imagine all the things you've ever said you'd do to get yourself closer to the future direction you desire. In my case, I've said I'd work out every morning. I've said I'd generate leads on speaking engagements every Monday. I've said I'd do video blogs twice a week. I've said that I'll write out my small goals on the first Sunday of every month. I haven't stuck with any of these things. None of 'em. Because we're all human and even our grand plans to be consistent can fail us.

How many times have you ever said you'd work on a dream over the weekend? Then when that weekend comes, you also get invited for last-minute plans with your friends. So you go hang out with them instead, and you proceed to spend the following days lamenting your decision because now you'll have to wait until next weekend to work on your dream. It was a small plan that would have brought you closer to the future you wanted if you'd just kept it and said no, trusting future you with your future dreams. Look, sometimes procrastination does pay off—because you're energetically not ready, because it's not time yet—but in moments like these you're just not prioritizing your small plans.

Research shows that people who envision the feelings of their future self show more self-control, and as the psychologist who ran this study notes, stepping into the shoes of our future selves helps us to realize both the positive and negative ramifications of our decisions. Committing to small actions becomes easier when I tap into future me. It's helpful to think about how great it will make her feel, and to promise to uphold her happiness. I try to trust that future me will be consistent too.

Your future self has so much to share with you if you can try to communicate with her and step into how she would feel about the choices in front of you. Would she be *so* happy you spent the money on that vacation to prevent burnout? Would she be really proud that you spent your mornings building out that business plan instead of hitting SNOOZE? Would she be grateful that you pushed past your discomfort to let some of those toxic situations go?

On the morning before a friend's wedding in Ojai, California, I went up to the region's Meditation Mount and did just that. I stepped into my future self about a year from that day. What would make her feel proud to be standing there that day? What had I done between now and then that was giving her great joy? What things had I created, continued, or stopped doing consistently that honored a year-older me?

The answers were impossibly small plans. Pretty easy. And above all else, I could feel their truth. It was so clear what I needed to do to honor her, my future self. And something about that clarity brought so much motivation and a whole list of short-term, tiny plans that I began working on and implementing immediately. And I haven't stopped since.

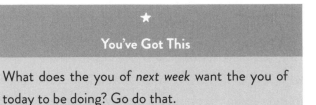

What does the you of *next week* want the you of today to be doing? Go do that.

JUST KEEP GOING

When I reflect on the things I'm the most proud of, sticking with my small plans like writing on my blog in those early years is really high on that list. Doing the things that nobody saw, nobody was congratulating me for, nobody read, but writing because it energized me and because I trusted that my commitment was leading me somewhere? That fills me with pride.

The most successful people I know have just stuck with their ambitions, whatever those were—designing, selling, making, baking, creating. They just kept going, like little engines that could, when there was no glamour or accolades. They kept going with their small plans. Because here's what happens when you stick with those small achievements: They grow. They get bigger. Stone by stone, they create the pyramid of your dreams.

It sounds so easy, but sometimes future success comes from being the person who just didn't stop. Being the person who believed in themselves and in what they were creating enough to simply continue. How many people have told you they were starting something and maybe they did it for a minute, or a month or two, and then slowly it faded away? On the other hand, if you pick the most successful person you know and look at their path, there's always something that they just kept doing. There's a path they just kept marching on. They kept going. It may not have ended how it started, and it may not have been linear, but the point is that they're still going. They recalibrated and just kept doing it.

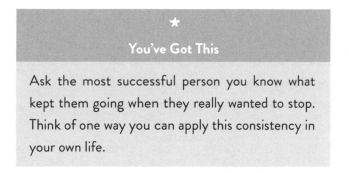

★

You've Got This

Ask the most successful person you know what kept them going when they really wanted to stop. Think of one way you can apply this consistency in your own life.

THE LIE OF THE BIG LEAP

When you think about getting to where you're going, or when you hear about the people who have, there's so much emphasis on the single, life-changing moment when everything came together, the giant plan that made it all happen. The day someone quit their job and went all in on their dream. The day they pitched their crazy idea. Or when they finally put their hat in the ring for that huge promotion that changed their whole life.

Those moments are all real. I have had a few of them myself. But they're not the whole story. You don't have to upend your life to be living it. You don't have to risk it all immediately to get what you're hoping for. Big leaps don't guarantee you getting to your desired future faster.

Quite the contrary, I believe there isn't really any such thing as the big leap. It's total bullshit. Rather, the big leap is an inflection point that happens to be preceded by a long series of small steps and tiny plans.

Think about running a marathon. You've taken how many steps? Let's say thirty-three thousand. And it's not until that final step that you cross the finish line. Was the last step any different from the first one? Other than you feeling much more tired, no, it just happens to be the one step with a little bit more specialness because it's the step that got you to the end, the same but different from the 32,999 steps before it. The big finish didn't happen as a result of one massive leap. You didn't long-jump the marathon. Rather, it was the result of small step after small step for 26.2 miles of torture (or at least that's how it felt for me).

"Overnight successes" are almost always ten years in the making and filled with these tiny steps. How long was Kendra Scott running businesses before her jewelry line took off? How long was Kerry Washington acting before anyone knew her name? The answer, despite the details: a long time.

But they kept going. They kept creating. And they had been executing on their small plans a seriously long time before they ever hit that inflection point.

What's important is to be all in on your commitment to yourself and to your bite-size plans, regardless of whether any recognition is coming your way. It's not about making massive changes that require you to upend your life. Gradual is a beautiful thing. Gradual builds. Gradual allows you to adjust. Gradual allows you to change and re-fine. Your energy and daily actions can be all in without your *how* being abrupt or hasty.

CELEBRATION KEEPS THE SMALL PLANS COMIN'

But there's still so much left to do. This is the dreamer's main reason for not taking small, achieved plans seriously or getting excited about them. *There's still so much to do* is the sentiment used to *not* get excited, to *not* celebrate, to *not* be proud of what's been done.

Well, screw that. Of course there's way more to do. There will *always* be so much left to do. But at some point you have to look at the meaningful steps you've taken and be proud of them. Find grati-tude and excitement in them. And don't always obsess over what's still left to do.

We all do it. We move mountains and completely forget that we ever touched them. We create magic and move on. We do seriously awesome shit, however small, and don't celebrate.

Well, reflecting and celebrating is where it's actually at. When you take the time to reflect on and celebrate what's happened, you create a landslide of self-belief. Whatever in your life is going right, cele-brate it. It doesn't matter what win you had today and it doesn't mat-ter how small the plan was—sending that cold email, finishing the next lesson in your online course, tinkering with a camera, initiating a meeting, redoing your résumé, or writing a blog post—you've got to celebrate it and acknowledge what you've done.

Take inventory of what you do. There will always be a list longer than the Mississippi waiting for your attention. But with each thing you've accomplished, big and small, c e l e b r a t e . . . *yourself.*

You've got to learn to toot your own horn. Trust me, on the path to your desired direction, no one is going to come put a sparkly party hat on your head and throw you a celebration. You've got to congratulate yourself and host your own party. And it's totally possible to do this without being a narcissistic asshole. When you're celebrating your small wins, *acknowledge who helped make it happen.* Because success is a team sport. We don't do any of this alone. So take credit where it's due for you, and thank the people who might have helped you do it. It'll deepen the network and community that you're a part of.

And be real about what it took. Celebrating is awesome. Celebrating little things is awesome. But that awesomeness took some bullshit, it took some challenges, and it probably took a healthy dose of doubt. Open up about that stuff. It doesn't mean being self-deprecating. It doesn't mean being negative about the celebration or the win. It simply means sharing the journey that goes along with this highlight.

This cycle of celebration, when the feeling is right, will infuse energy and momentum into the progress of your small plans. It'll give you more excitement to dig in and to keep going. It'll give you a moment of pause so you stop obsessing over where you're not for a hot second to be where your feet are—and to be excited about that.

WORKSHEET
The Small Plans Plan

I've said before that I'm a reformed goal junkie. So the last thing I'm going to do is throw you into another five-year-plan goal-setting worksheet. Rather, we're going to get down to the nitty-gritty on what feels good right now, so that you can feel really good later. It'll be small. So get ready.

Close your eyes and imagine the best version of yourself. What does that person do in a day, every day? Think about the habits that are most aligned with what you want to be doing or who you want to be, then answer the following questions.

What do you do to feel calm?

What do you do to feel healthy?

What do you do to feel productive?

```
........................................................................
:                                                                      :
:                                                                      :
:                                                                      :
:                                                                      :
........................................................................
```

What do you do to feel love?

```
........................................................................
:                                                                      :
:                                                                      :
:                                                                      :
:                                                                      :
........................................................................
```

What do you do to feel joy?

```
........................................................................
:                                                                      :
:                                                                      :
:                                                                      :
:                                                                      :
........................................................................
```

Small habits are small plans. And they matter because they give us the energy to take on and create the future we desire most. Are your habits aligned with what you want to do and be?

WORKSHEET
Trickle Back

Imagine yourself one year from today. This is the future you who feels on fire, completely confident, and like she's actively creating the path for herself that she cares most about. Now ask this future you who is calm, clear about her direction, and joyous: What needs to be done in the next year in order for you to feel that way?

Do It Now

What are three things you could do this week to help make that a possibility?

1.

2.

3.

CHAPTER 9

Bewitch Yourself

Kind words can be short and easy to speak,
but their echoes are truly endless.

—MOTHER TERESA

WORDS CARRY EPIC WEIGHT. With them, you can create a world of turmoil for yourself. Or you can create one of positivity and purpose.

So much of building self-belief relies on what words you're saying to yourself and what kinds of messages you choose to let your spirit feed on. These words help your small actions gain even more momentum. Those thoughts of yours are there when you wake up and there when you eat and there when you breathe and there when you're trying to fall asleep. Words can create realities both true and untrue. Words can be your magic wand or your atomic bomb.

The fortunate part is, *you decide.* You have full ownership over which words are on repeat in your head. You have agency over what comes out of your mouth. It's all in your power.

When you start creating plans, even the smallest of them, and trying things out, the story you tell both about yourself to the world and to yourself about the world is your own kind of magic—even when you don't know where those plans will drop you.

You get to decide what a single event actually means to you. That meaning is the story you tell. I learned this at an early age because my mother always told us, "You decide which side of the bed you wake up on." *And ain't that the truth.* Imagine splashing coffee all over your outfit in the morning, signifying what is surely going to be a bad day. Once you decide as much, you end up looking for the negative in everything that happens. Perhaps not so coincidentally, it really does become a bad day. Or . . . you can decide to shrug it off, give it no meaning, and continue on with your day.

We get to decide what the events in our life mean to us. Technically, no event means anything until we attribute a meaning to it. So why not attribute positive meaning and thought to the events in your life? Instead of being apocalyptic about every little thing that happens to you, what if you just let things slide off?

Given, some events can be much harder to spin positively than others.

Whenever I'm in the thick of something I want to bitch or complain about, I remember that the way I talk about what's happening, and who I tell, and how big a deal I make out of it in my head and with my words is all up to me. Which is probably why in 2011 when I loathed about 99 percent of my work at the time, I perked right up when this parable was emailed to me:

A man came across three masons who were working at chipping chunks of granite from large blocks. The first seemed unhappy with his job, chipping away and frequently looking at his watch.

When the man asked what he was doing, the first mason responded, rather curtly, "I'm hammering this stupid rock, and I can't wait till five when I can go home."

A second mason, seemingly more interested in his work, was hammering diligently and when asked what he was doing, answered, "Well, I'm molding this block of rock so that it can be used with others to construct a wall. It's not bad work, but I'll sure be glad when it's done."

A third mason was hammering at his block fervently, taking time to stand back and admire his work. He chipped off small pieces until he was satisfied that it was the best he could do. When he was questioned about his work he stopped, gazed skyward, and proudly proclaimed, "I'm building a cathedral!"[1]

This parable has always stuck with me as a reminder to consider the story I'm telling myself and others about my own circumstances, because the circumstances I loathed in 2011 were actually building blocks for my cathedral of today. Day in and day out I was getting a step closer to finding my way. If I could have trusted that such misery was leading me here—instead of being so negative—I could have helped ease my own frustration.

But I know—like, knooooow—it's a *battle* to keep your attitude above the line of positivity in this way. Especially with your frustrated thoughts doing laps in your head. Everyone touts "positive thinking," but have we addressed how damn hard that actually is? Left to our own devices, we think at a rate of thirteen hundred words a minute,[2] and it's said that 90 percent of our thoughts are repetitive.[3] So if any percentage of those are negative, think about just *how many* negative words are going through your head at any given time if you're not thoughtful about it.

But the negativity that literally all of us experience isn't our fault. We don't have these feelings because we're some pissy creatures who enjoy pessimistic patterns. It's because the brain is actually wired with a negativity bias so that we're hyperaware of any threats to our surroundings. We actually experience negative events more intensely than we do positive ones. They're imprinted on our brains with more significance and we naturally pay more attention to the bad stuff. While that was surely helpful in the caveman days, now our safety is threatened more by the decision to cross the street buried in our phones than by an aggressive animal charging our village.[4]

Luckily, we have some control over changing this bias toward negativity. While the brain is an organ and not a muscle, it can be trained to improve, learn, and change itself much like one. Like with muscle memory, your brain can be taught to fire certain ways without thinking too much, by harnessing its plasticity (as in its ability to change).[5] Consider all the times you go on total autopilot, whether it's navigating home, doing your makeup, or washing the dishes. When you do things that you've done a million times, you don't even have to think about them. You do them, successfully, while not really paying attention to what you're doing. The same works for making the choice to be more positive with your thoughts, your reactions, and your words. At first it'll require focus, but then it will become second nature because your brain becomes used to firing in that way.

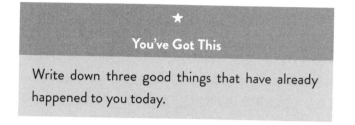

★

You've Got This

Write down three good things that have already happened to you today.

YOU NEED YOURSELF

No matter how many pep talks someone gives you or how much inspiration you read on the internet, there's only one voice that truly matters: yours. Because no matter what's happening in your life, the only person in your head is you. There is no one else who can control your thoughts but you. No one else's positive words matter if you're regularly and continually ripping yourself apart with negative chatter. And no, this isn't just a Pollyanna prescription to think positive. It's a call to get you into the right mindset so you *act* positive. That's all that actually matters.

You need yourself. And stepping into the small actions that fuel your confidence will get massively easier when you find a way to soften your inner bitch.

I think most of us take the voice in our head for granted. We don't think to challenge it. We don't realize that it can be changed. We don't know that it doesn't have to be that way. I remember that the first time I noticed it was in middle school. Every morning when I'd be in the bathroom brushing my teeth and doing my hair, I'd feel like my thoughts ran a mile a minute and were blaring through a megaphone. They felt louder than during the rest of the day, and they weren't always nice thoughts. I noticed the voice then, but it would take another decade before I'd begin working to make the voice sweeter, more supportive, and (hopefully) less anxious. But it took me landing on a faraway island and meeting a fifty-year-old Australian healer to get there. He doesn't call himself a healer, but I do.

In one of my first sessions with Healer Jim, he asked me to think about two different situations: someone I love getting in my face and saying "Fuck you" with meaning; and that same person getting in my face and saying "I love you" with meaning. Even just imagining the scenario, I could feel the difference in my body. You change two words and the difference is an entire world of emotion. It was a significant lesson in paying attention to the power of words, because they not only create our reality, they create our feelings about our reality.

Before I knew it he had me driving around the island on my scooter repeating, "I love and approve of myself." Each week became a different lesson in words. I'd walk out with a new phrase to focus on, written on little business cards in scratchy ballpoint pen that I still keep in my wallet today. From the mirror to the surfboard, everywhere I went, I paid attention to the voice in my head and came back to Healer Jim's affirmative sentences when I noticed things going astray. They were like guardrails to get my thoughts back on track, and most important, I could feel the relaxation in my body and the release of unhelpful energy as I adjusted my thinking. There was a shift that came from being on my own team, instead of constantly against myself.

And it's why on any given day, I've got a rotating selection of positive sentences on repeat in my head, plus a daily calendar notification that pops up at five p.m. with a few positive sentences to get my mind in check regardless of what's going wrong.

The words happening in your head only have as much power as you give them. The negative shit isn't going to go away, but you can course-correct by putting some more positive thoughts and words into your day. I've come to realize it's one of the not-so-talked-about secret strategies of people doing big things. They *know* that their thoughts aren't always on their side, but they act anyway. And they can do that because they know how to quiet the crap and magnify their strength.

If you're not sure what sentence will get you going when the going is tough, here are some go-to self–pep talks you can borrow:

Me: "Trust the process."

Jaclyn Johnson: "Nothing really matters. In five years who will care?"

Carly Heitlinger: "This too shall pass."

Tiffany Dufu: "If you want what you've never had before, you're going to have to do something you've never done before in order to get it."

Marah Lidey: "Know your power."

Ashley Longshore: "Girl, I love you and I would totally fuck you."

A BREAKFAST OF QUEENS

It's no surprise to me that those middle school mornings doing my hair were the first time I realized there was a negative and critical monologue going on in my head. I've always been sensitive to mornings—how I start them, how I spend my time, what I look at, what I engage with. Do I wake up and engage in actions that get my angsty brain going? Or do I give myself space to revel in the beauty of the moment? Most times it's the former, but I'm trying like hell for it to regularly be the latter. Because research shows that how you start the day really does affect the rest of it, like how much you get done and how well you do it. Your mood in the morning affects your performance for the rest of the day.[6]

I've learned the hard way that I have to be super picky with what I choose to look at on my phone in the morning. Which means no social scrolling and no email checking until I'm actually ready to sit down and work. But there is one message I always count on to give me an early pick-me-up.

When I learned about what my friend Naomi Hirabayashi was launching with her former colleague and business partner, Marah Lidey, I knew it was my new favorite thing. A daily text message service to address negative thought patterns? Yup, yup, me, I'm in. My morning needed this. And of course I was in, because with Shine Text, Naomi and Marah were creating a solution based on an experience we all have: feeling as if our own insecurities and false beliefs are doing laps in our heads.

"That voice will always be there," Marah told me. "You have to figure out how it will work with you as opposed to against you. But it's never black and white. It's never like 'Now my inner voice is chill.'"

Your expectation shouldn't be that your negative thoughts fully disappear one day. That inner voice is never going to be perfectly calm and it's sure never fully going away. Which is why Marah and Naomi both wanted to create something to help us act confidently despite all that and, importantly, take all of our feelings and thoughts in stride. Because they're normal. And a part of the process.

"The goal isn't to train ourselves happy," Naomi shared with me. "With success comes greater expectations, and you have to be kind to yourself about that adjustment, which means growth. It's not about being happy all the time."

So don't hear "positive" and think you're supposed to be positive constantly. Don't hear it and think *positive or else, positive or bust.* But do become a witness to your thoughts and understand that your feelings and thoughts are normal. How can you still act despite any of those negative thoughts?

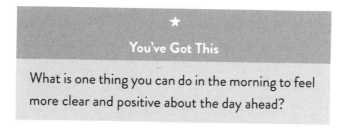

★

You've Got This

What is one thing you can do in the morning to feel more clear and positive about the day ahead?

WHEN TOO MUCH IS TOO MUCH

Words, thoughts, your mind . . . they play a *major* role in making your decisions. Do you stay or do you go? Do you create or do you wait? Do you say it or do you mute it? Do you write it? Do you book? Do you sell? Do you? Should you? Can you?

You've likely always been told not to rush big decisions. You've been told to give them *plenty* of thought. To weigh all of your options, and to let them breathe. But like anything, there's a really fine line between giving something some thought and turning that into straight rumination—which is rehashing, fixating, or obsessing over any one thought or problem. The kicker is, with ruminating you keep thinking about it, but you don't *do* anything to solve it.

Ruminating on a problem, decision, or action is *not* helping you. It's hindering you big-time. Double big-time. Ruminating on something is like taking a baby step down the dungeon of lack of confidence. Being decisive, on the other hand, fuels confidence.

I know, I know, I know, you're probably thinking what I used to think: *Well, how can I decide if I don't know what to decide? Isn't that chicken and egg?* Well, many times trying to decide isn't helpful thinking. It's just obsessive worry. And to tell the difference, you just have to ask yourself, "Is this helpful? Am I creating solutions with these thoughts?" Many, many, many times the answer is no. And if you're not in a position to do something about deciding, stop yourself from considering it. Oftentimes, we make powerful decisions when we're doing something other than trying to decide.

> ★
> ### You've Got This
>
> What is a problem, decision, or worry that you've been *majorly* overthinking? What's one small action you can take instead of thinking about that?

When it comes to stopping that rumination cycle and trusting ourselves, our bodies can tell us *a lot*. If we chill out and feel a decision instead of overthinking it, we can find clarity that we wouldn't have otherwise found. We all have an important intelligence system that responds based not on what we can think and figure out with our minds, but on what we can feel in our bodies. Some scientists have nicknamed this the "second brain," and it's a network of neurons that extensively lines our gut. And our emotions are very much impacted by those nerves in our gut.[7]

To figure out what I should do anytime I'm ruminating, I employ a strategy for getting to the root of how to move forward. I make a decision (without actually doing anything about it). Then I lie in a quiet space (I love lying horizontally on my bed, but the floor works beautifully too), imagining that I'm in the life that that decision holds. I stay there and observe how that decision feels in my body. Does it *feel* right, future aside, past aside, judgments aside? What is my body telling me that's the same as or different from the shit my brain likes to prop up?

You can rinse and repeat this with a different decision to compare how it all feels.

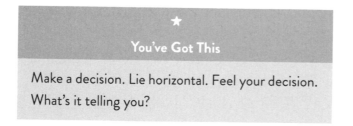

★
You've Got This

Make a decision. Lie horizontal. Feel your decision. What's it telling you?

SETTLING (YUP, I SAID IT)

Some of the best decisions you can make will happen when you don't give them too much thought about the perfect outcome and settle instead for good enough. Sometimes when you feel inspired to act boldly on one of your plans, you've just got to do something that can't be undone. Otherwise, you leave too much space for fear and anxiety to run the show.

You're able to take bold action when you make decisions that are good enough rather than perfect, because holding out for perfect is holding you back, way back. It freezes you up, because it's not actually that you want to be perfect, it's that you obsessively want to avoid any kind of mistake. But success doesn't come from avoiding mistakes, because no decision will ever hold a perfect outcome. And no decision we make will ever be flawless. Most people dominating in any given field, believe it or not, are less likely to be qualified as perfectionists.[8] The reason for this is that all that swirl of worry, anxiety, and hoping that this is the "perfect" decision—meaning one that doesn't lead to failure—gets in the way of deciding, of moving, of acting.

> **Holding out for perfect is holding you back.**

So a great way to develop your confidence in deciding when the deciding is hard is to pick something that will work for now. This will actually reduce your stress and help you feel more in control.[9]

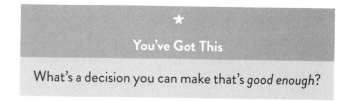

★

You've Got This

What's a decision you can make that's *good enough?*

And an important note: Doing nothing is a decision too. Swift action isn't always the right decision. The decision can be to stay. The decision can absolutely be to leave. The decision can 100 percent be to decide on what not to do.

YOUR WORDS CREATE OTHERS' PERCEPTIONS TOO

Have you ever met someone at a cocktail party who spent a few too many minutes telling you about their drab job that they've been in forever but don't actually love? They're a banker, they say. But their *real* dream, the *real* real, is to start a music production company, and they spend most of their waking moments when they're not at their day job working with artists to record new, interesting tunes.

OK, maybe that exact conversation hasn't happened to you, but whenever I hear some version of this, I'm always left wondering . . . why didn't they just tell me they're a producer? Because they *are* producing and owning that identity, and that really matters. You're allowed to care about and be things that may not pay you the big bucks right now or ever.

I know how torturous it can feel when you're stumbling to explain who you are, what you do, or what you care about. Torturous. There's this internal dialogue that goes round and round and round that says, *They think I'm cray. They don't get it. I sound dumb. This is confusing. Etc., etc., etc.* And you feel defeated before the conversation has even gotten into swing. Which is so precisely and exactly why having a language for yourself that makes you excited and energized really matters.

It took me a long time to own that I was more than the job I was doing. That my identity wasn't wrapped up in a job title. That my future actually may just be doing what I love to do the most. None of that clicked until I overheard my parents trying to explain what I do (love me some Real McCoys, but they crashed and burned), and I realized it could be much simpler. "What I do" could be so much closer to my heart. I write and speak. And that was that. It was like my future clicked in that moment, because I was owning with my words what I wanted to do, and the opportunities that aligned themselves with that desire began finding me quicker than they ever had before.

The decisions you're making about where you're going next don't have to be hidden. Owning your future, the identity you're working on, the path you want to expand, doesn't start once it's in full swing. It doesn't happen when it's validated by someone else. It happens right now, through you. Use your words to put a stake in the ground on what you actually care about and spend your time on, and the world will rise to meet it.

You can't change your life in an instant. But you *can* change how you talk about your life, and that's enough to begin shifting your entire world. Being energized by your own description of who you are and what you're doing matters. Really matters. Because when you say it, you will start to believe it. When you own it, you'll feel it. As will others.

Please, don't keep your dreams in hiding.

WORKSHEET
FROM–TO

The language you use to talk about yourself sends a message to you and to others regarding what you're really about. But do you ever take the time to figure out those powerful messages?

FROM

If someone at a networking event said, "So tell me about yourself," how would you respond?

TO

Now, let's create an answer that really resonates with you and who you are.

What do you care about most?

How do you spend your free time?

What activities make you feel the most inspired?

What are you best in the world at?

Next time you have the chance to tell someone about yourself, use language from these answers to really show them what makes you *you*. Powerful words equal powerful outcomes.

CHAPTER 10

Scared Shitless and Still You'll Shine

you will be lost and unlost. over and over again.
relax love. you were meant to be
this glorious. epic. story.
—Nayyirah Waheed

Left untamed, our minds can become theaters of fear, especially when we're taking steps into the unknown. Everywhere we look and all that we imagine turns into a mile-high brick wall created by terror. It feels so real. Frequently, we believe what that fear has to say. Which is why so often we're told to simply cast it away completely, like that's the only pathway forward: *Be fearless! Conquer your fears!*

Loads of bullshit. It perpetuates a belief about fear that most of us get wrong. Fear is not something that goes away. It's not something that even diminishes, really. Rather, it stays. You can simply become better and better at hearing it without listening.

That's the goal: **to hear without listening**. Kind of like all those times you were playing your favorite game as a kid while your mom or dad yelled from the kitchen to go clean your room. *Yeah, yeah, yeah,* you thought. But then you didn't budge, because you were hearing it, but you sure weren't listening.

The best way to handle fear is to let it be the voice in the other room. Let it give you something for consideration. Let it create some cold sweats. Let it even cause you to pause. But then go on with your day, your plan, your dream. Don't listen. And whatever you do, don't believe what it says.

Fear and doubt feel similar and often happen at the same time, but they are actually quite different. Doubt comes about when we're unsure about ourselves and what we're doing. Fear turns on when we think there's real failure or dire consequences on the other side of our actions. And the riskier our ideas may be, the louder and more intense that fear can get.

Because fear will tell you all kinds of crazy shit. It'll tell you that you're absolutely going to fail, miserably. That you'll fall flat on your face. That you'll never work this out. That everyone will laugh at you. That you'll never make it. That you'll end up hungry, homeless, and embarrassed. Fear will attempt to convince you that your worst nightmares will come true about this thing that you're wanting to try, to put out there, to create.

However, you can't let fear keep you small. As you're making your small plans and doing something about them, you'll expand. You will. And as you start to step into bigger and bigger ideas, and develop confidence that pushes you to take bigger and bigger steps, fear will be there riding shotty. But acting despite your fears will grow your confidence. All the small steps you take that scare the crap out of you prepare you for the big step, the one that begins to really clear your path wide open.

I experienced all sorts of small fears on my way here. I acknowledged that they scared me. But I knew I could handle them. Letting people read my writing, being interviewed by press, holding a mic with lots of faces staring back at me, I was full of both doubts and big fears. What I didn't know was that powering on would prepare me for an even bigger risk, the biggest one yet.

I had shown up in Denver after one too many weeks of stress and travel. I didn't want to be there, but I needed to be there. I had to be there. On the way in from the airport I'd taken a call that is completely insignificant now. But when I hung up and threw my phone into my bag, I looked out the window and thought, *I don't want to be doing this anymore.* And the response I got from the back of my mind was a loud whisper that I felt all the way to my toes, impossibly clear: *So don't. You're ready. You've been ready. Go to Bali or India. Pack up your stuff. Give it away. And go. Go launch your business and step into your dream.*

Pack up? Bali? India? Business?

I'd contemplated running my own business before, but that was about it. Clearly, my subconscious had known how quickly I'd make all of this happen way before I did, because I had already been working with an executive coach with the intention of running my own business eventually.

While I was surprised by the whispering thought, I felt the terror of its truth. One layer below that terror was excitement so big I could cry. In my heart, though, it was a truth I couldn't unhear. It brought clarity to every part of my cells. It wasn't just a truth; it was *my* truth. In a single whisper I got a blinding, momentary look into my future. It sounded crazy—batshit, actually (still does!)—but it felt so right. But sweet terror, I'd have to unravel my life in order to make this happen and to follow the truth.

It meant giving up my San Francisco apartment. It meant leaving a job I cared about deeply. It meant purging my things. It meant showing up alone in a foreign country. It meant starting a business I didn't know how to run. It meant undoing my financial security net. It meant the most insane amount of unknown I've ever had the capacity to imagine in my life.

Imagining the unknown is like watching wind: You can't see what you're meant to feel. It's a waste of time. The unknown will always (forever and ever) be there. There's no beating it. The only chance any of us have is to learn to live hand in hand with that fear of what's next, making the most of today with the hope it'll all turn out OK tomorrow.

For the next three days in Denver, I barely got through them without thinking about my whispered directive, and I spent the wee hours of the night googling everything I could about how to make this idea real. It was haunting me like a friendly ghost. I couldn't shake it, but I also sort of didn't want to. I was mesmerized.

I made a call to my wise work wife, Ellen, who told me exactly what I needed to hear: "Will there ever be a better time to do this? Life will only get more complex, so follow this feeling now." *OK. OK. I might actually be going for it*, I thought. And because life has some wild timing, I was already scheduled to see my executive business coach, Michèle, immediately upon landing home in San Francisco. So I rolled in with my suitcase, sat down, and couldn't believe what was about to come out of my mouth.

"I think I'm going to quit my job, move to Bali, and launch my business."

Bali because it's where I heard to go in the whisper. Bali because it's a beautiful and creative place that's also supposed to be quite cheap. Bali because it just felt right, even though I'd never visited. She listened to the entire story, and said she'd known this was what was ahead for me, that all of my plans to start my own business three to five years from now were three to five years too delayed. "You needed to see that for yourself, though," she said.

She asked, "What's stopping you?" *I'm scared shitless.* "Shitless" actually didn't even cover it at the time. The fear had wrapped me like a boa constrictor. I knew I couldn't ignore this, but I also couldn't answer it. Together, we walked through everything I was scared of. She had me go all the way down the rabbit hole of fear. "What are you worried will happen? What are you scared of, exactly?"

I'll end up broke.

I'll never be able to move back to San Francisco, the place I love.

Bali will be the worst.

Levo will think I'm ungrateful.

My dream won't work out. I'll have to find a new one.

I can't actually make money doing this.

People will say shit. Or they'll think I'm crazy.

I'll have to ask my parents for a couch to sleep on.

"Is any of it *that* bad? Is any of it life-threatening?" she asked.

"No. No, it's actually not that bad," I responded. Because the very worst thing that would happen—which I wouldn't like but I could definitely do—is that I'd have to get a full-time job somewhere working for someone.

Fear is pretty cowardly. As soon as you acknowledge it and look it

> The goal isn't to be fearless. The goal is to keep fear from running the show.

in the eye, it loses its power. It pretends to be this big secret, but once it sees the light, it loses that hold. The goal isn't to be fearless. The goal is to keep fear from running the show—your show.

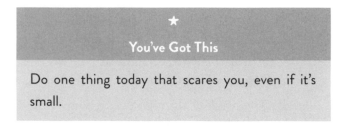

★

You've Got This

Do one thing today that scares you, even if it's small.

Here's what *did* happen because I felt the fear but didn't let it stop me:

* I transitioned from my full-time job into a part-time role.
* I ended up living most of that year in Bali writing, getting space, and laying the groundwork for my future.
* I gave away almost everything I owned. All that was left were a couple of boxes, my suitcase, and my violin.
* I launched my business and opened up a new path for myself.

And all those things put me on a fast track to here. Fear lost its power, but I gained mine.

And more than anything, making those changes and *believing* that I could do it, that I could figure it out, that I had the power? You never forget that kind of power once you've summoned it. It gives you the confidence to be bold again, and again, and again. You show yourself that following your truth will work out, and that self-belief will support you now and in the future.

INTO THE ARENA

Not everyone will like where you're headed and your ability to face your fears. This newfound direction and confidence, the one created by the compass of *you*, might give people plenty to talk about. And trust me, everyone will have their opinions. When your little light of belief turns on, it'll be noticeable. You might even seem like you've changed just a bit—because you're more sure, because you're doing things differently, because the world of possibility reflects back from your eyes—and there might be voices that try to make you small. Like with the voice of fear, you don't have to listen.

It is not the critic who counts; not the man who points out how the strong man stumbles, or where the doer of deeds could have done them better. The credit belongs to the man who is actually in the arena, whose face is marred by dust and sweat and blood; who strives valiantly; who errs, who comes up short again and again, because there is no effort without error and shortcoming; but who does actually strive to do the deeds; who knows great enthusiasms, the great devotions; who spends himself in a worthy cause; who at the best knows in the end the triumph of high achievement, and who at the worst, if he fails, at least fails while daring greatly, so that his place shall never be with those cold and timid souls who neither know victory nor defeat.

—THEODORE ROOSEVELT

When I first heard Brené Brown share this quote during her TED Talk on vulnerability, I wept. Because it's true. Because sometimes following the path of your dream hurts. Because often trusting yourself and your truth can be isolating, but it's always worth it.

There are so many different reasons we all stay out of "the arena," but that willingness to open ourselves up to failure and criticism in pursuit of our most expressed selves is where confidence is bred. As you continue to put one foot in front of the other in the face of fear or doubters, you stop playing someone else's version of the game. You begin to buck other people's expectations of you. Because you are *finally* tuning in to those little voices and excitements that have always been there, which requires you to step beyond the boundaries you or others set for you.

A few months after launching my business, I came across trolls on the internet talking about me. Well, more like an entire message board of trolls. They were saying rude things about me, and one even uploaded my photo with a nasty comment attached. I wasn't surprised this happened, because I'd seen it happen to one of my dearest blogger friends, but I was very surprised it was happening to little-ol'-just-launched me. As I glanced over the words on the page, my eyes immediately bugged out, my chest tightened, and I shut down that browser faster than lightning.

What in the actual fuck? was the first thing that went through my head. *Is what they're saying true?* was the next thing. And then I had a surge of anxiety about everything they'd said. Because naturally my brain only paid attention to whatever I was already worried or insecure about. Everything else rolled right off my back.

I gave myself about two seconds to decide: Do I run with my hurt feelings, or do I look at this differently?

While never a good thing, because internet bullying is awful and causes real damage to those on the receiving end, these trolls existing meant I had put myself and my work out there. And that's what I chose to focus on. It was a sign that I wasn't letting anything keep me small, especially my fear of what other people thought.

Finding your path requires being on the path. It requires being seen. And when you do that, all the people on the sidelines watching you live from a place of confidence and courage will have a front-row seat to what you're doing. They might heckle. They might throw popcorn. They might try to boo you off or drag you down. And they might wonder why you're even there. However, believing in yourself doesn't begin or end with their comments. It's built by what you do in the face of them. I'm not asking you to simply not care what other people think; that's way easier said than done. I'm asking you to continue putting yourself out there. When the doubts from the outside (or inside) come, think back to a few things you've done really well and let that ignite confidence in your future steps.

Whether these are people you've never met or people you've known your whole life, if they're not in the arena with you, don't listen to them.

Because what's true is that the people worth having in your corner will always support your rise, not amplify your fears.

MISTAKES BABY, MISTAKES

No doubt, you're gonna screw up. It's a by-product of taking action, which is required to build your confidence. Trust me when I say, there will be plenty of missteps.

You might accidentally send out a test email to your entire subscriber list, announcing the launch of your business that isn't launched yet. (Me.)

You might have to redo deliverables because you didn't fully read the terms of a contract. (Me.)

You might get screwed over in a business deal because you trusted a recommendation and ignored your gut feeling about someone. (Me.)

You might get onstage and say a celebrity's name completely wrong even though you practiced it a million times out loud backstage. (Also me.)

You might plan a major press event at an all-women's club and realize only hours before it's supposed to begin that the key people coming are men and not allowed in. (Unfortunately, me.)

You'll spell things wrong. You'll quote things wrong. You'll say things wrong. You'll do things completely wrong. You'll get frustrated. You'll say things you didn't mean. You'll overreact.

But those mistakes aren't signs you shouldn't be doing this. Not at all. These mistakes are signs that you're trying and learning and growing. All mistakes are practice. The forced errors are signs of effort. Whether they were small ones, major ones, or deal-breaker ones, they'll keep happening to teach you something. Your fear will make them seem way bigger than they are. But the truth of a mistake is that you were *trying*, and your resilience will bring you back from all the shit feelings to keep you keeping on.

Remember, there's no way to learn what you're capable of unless you're testing your limits and making mistakes.

Getting back up is key. Lessons can't be learned unless you get your ass off the ground to see what's dusted, what's broken, how you feel, and how you'll move forward. There will always be crap feelings of fear after a mistake. And there will always be a lesson to learn. There might even be an apology that needs to be made. And definitely responsibility to be taken.

> There's no way to learn what you're capable of unless you're testing your limits and making mistakes.

Mistakes aren't what you think.

A mistake is not a price tag on your value.

It's not a sign to stop.

A mistake isn't the sum of your experience.

It doesn't mean you should give up.

You are not your mistake. Your mistake is a by-product of your effort, of your trying, of your ability to step off the sidelines and into the experience of your path so that you can find out what feels right for you and the direction you want to be taking.

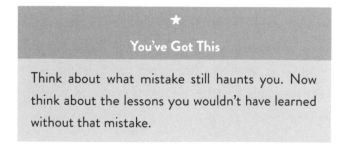

★

You've Got This

Think about what mistake still haunts you. Now think about the lessons you wouldn't have learned without that mistake.

YOUR BLIND SPOT

Fear is an attention whore. When fear comes into the picture it takes up all the space in your chest and in your mind. And it always shows up at the most inopportune times, the times when you so badly want to make progress, pick up momentum toward your future, and get moving forward, forward, and more forward.

Fear *wants* you to look at it and only it. It wants you to get lost in the forest of terrible feelings and believe all the apocalyptic obscenities that it screams at you while you do. And as it steals all of your dang attention, there's actually an entire other side of the coin that's being forgotten.

As you obsess over the negative what-ifs, you're totally missing the *positive* what-ifs.

What if this next step opens up a future beyond your wildest dreams?

What if that pitch is your big break?

What if that piece you write goes viral?

What if showing up at that dinner that you *really* don't want to go to is the key to discovering your next big job?

Possibility is a powerful thing. But if you're so wrapped up in all the reasons why you're scared or unsure because you're listening to fear, it's much harder to get yourself into a place that sees the sunshine in the sky instead of the black clouds. Believing in the beauty that's beyond those clouds of fear is what will help you tap into the power to act alongside fear, instead of stopping because of it.

MAKE IT A QUICKIE

When I showed up in Bali having fully dismantled the stability of my life, I had no idea what I was doing there. I had gotten through the fear that had gotten me there—all the tough conversations, the big changes, and the major decisions to uproot my life and jump into a new path. But still, intense fear continued to show up. On my first night there, I got up in the middle of the night, looked in the mirror, and thought, *What the fuck have you done?* The next morning, I spent the second day of the New Year lying on the beach writing my desires for what was ahead. But I couldn't shake the continuous *WTF am I doing here?* and *Have I just ruined my life?* fears. I didn't have so much as a place to live other than a hotel for a few nights. I didn't know how to ride a scooter, which was the primary mode of transport on the island. And my fear was crashing way harder than the waves in front of me.

It was then that I shut down my thoughts and picked up a book by Pema Chödrön. I found myself surprised when in it she explained that our feelings actually only last ninety seconds. Ninety seconds . . . that's it. I don't know about you, but when I'm in the throes of fear, it can last all day. Dr. Jill Bolte Taylor, a Harvard-trained brain scientist, lays out how this is possible in her book, *My Stroke of Insight: A Brain Scientist's Personal Journey*: "Once triggered, the chemical released by my brain surges through my body and I have a physiological experience. Within 90 seconds from the initial trigger, the chemical component of my anger has completely dissipated from my blood and my automatic response is over. If, however, I remain angry after those

90 seconds have passed, then it is because I have chosen to let that circuit continue to run."[1]

So, if a jolt of fear actually only lasts ninety seconds, then how is it that we spend so much time in the swirl?

Because of the things we make up in our heads. We get the fire of that scared feeling lit, and then we add gasoline to it with our own thoughts. We create our own bonfire of fear. It happens so fast.

Say you get excited about the idea of taking the lead on a new company project.

And then you think about enlisting your boss's help.

But you wonder what happens if you mess the project up.

Your boss will probably question your fit within the company.

Then, they'll decide they don't want you to be here at all.

Then they'll fire you.

And then you'll be jobless.

And homeless.

And your family and friends will think you're a failure.

And you'll never be able to come back from it.

And life is over, actually over.

Confirmed. Definitely not having that conversation.

That's how quickly it happens. That's how nervous fear over a conversation becomes an all-out assault and keeps you small. An idea becomes catastrophic when you let fear run the show. And then you take that to mean you have no choice but to just go with the flow of what's happening to you, instead of creating a future for yourself that you've chosen.

How often do you let fear run like this? How often do you let the shitty head space it takes you into leave you feeling helpless and dumb

for even thinking about the great inspiration you had? For even believing it might be a good idea?

Follow that feeling of being terrified by following through on
what triggered the fear in the first place. Because in the end, fear isn't
as scary as you let it seem. It's really just friendly friction occurring as
you move forward to where you want to be. You get to decide what to
do with that fear. Do you let it stop you completely? Or do you create
a masterpiece with the discomfort, much like an oyster does to create
a pearl?

When the proverbial grain of sand slips inside an oyster, it causes
major discomfort to the oyster's soft insides. To protect itself from the
irritation, the oyster begins layering smooth material called nacre
around the grain of sand. Slowly, coat after coat, layer after layer, a
beautiful pearl is formed.

Like the oyster, you want the irritation, the intruders, the discomfort of trespassing fear. Because with it, you'll create your master-
pieces. Step by step, the magic will unfold.

Contrary to what you might think, you can absolutely handle this.
No matter how loud your fear gets and how scared you might feel,
you've made it through 100 percent of your worst days up until this
point, and you'll make it through this moment, this feeling, this
month too. You will.

Now, no one can tell you if your fear is a real danger or if it is the
natural by-product of risk. But tune in to your gut; it knows. Most
times, when it comes to creating our future, the steps we're taking
equal change. And change feels like risk. And risk sets off the fighty
and flighty feelings. Know that it's happening, breathe deeply, and
remind yourself of your power. *You can handle this.*

WORKSHEET
Your Worst-Case Scenario

Think about a change you want to make, or a big step you want to take to free yourself from feeling lost—something you're pretty scared of.

Write out in excruciating detail all the worst things that could happen if you were to do that thing.

If these worst-case scenarios were to actually happen, could you handle it? And how?

Tell someone you trust about the step that scares you shitless. Speak that fear into the light. And then keep going.

CHAPTER 11

Encore

YOU NEVER KNOW who you're inspiring.

I heard that quote once in the middle of a sweaty spin class, and it's stayed with me over all these years. It's stayed so near to me because I believe it's so damn true.

And because it also includes us. As in, you never know that the person you're inspiring may also be . . . you. The beauty of getting to action, instead of waiting to feel all ready and sure and confident to do so, is that you'll create a powerful and virtuous cycle of doing that for yourself. A cycle of continually inspiring yourself, and inspiring yourself forward, step by step, foot by foot, when you most need it, toward the direction you've been searching for.

Whether you realize it or not, you're a role model for someone. Colleagues, friends, the little girl next door, or that faraway follower on social—your energy is casting a light somewhere that you may not

You won't always be lost,
but you'll always be
finding your way.

even see. This is the by-product of inspiring yourself, which is possibly even more important. When you create your way no matter how you feel, others who know you, meet you, or have come across your work will feel like they can move forward boldly as themselves too.

If you're thinking no one sees you, they do. You don't have to have audiences at scale following your every move to have an impact. It may be your younger sibling, the best friend doubting herself too, the colleague across the way, your clients, the people in your class, your parents' friends—your actions have the consequential effect of inspiring them, of showing them what self-belief looks like, of energizing them to believe in themselves too.

Because your life is a story for others. So let it be an expression of who you are, what you care about most, and how you live in that confidently. Let your life express an unwillingness to let any self-doubt keep you from moving forward.

Here's the real truth: You won't always be lost, but you'll always be finding your way.

There's really no destination to arrive at other than where you are. These steps—the turns, the twists, the really good, the really lost, the really fun, and the really confusing—they *are* the way. And with the tools you have now to believe in yourself through it all, you can actually enjoy the journey instead of letting the journey be dictated by the destination.

Finding your way is going to look different this year than it does next year. It'll look even more different five years from now. And none of it will go as you planned. Your path will not be a perfect succession of events.

Because nothing about your life is linear. Your work will not be linear. Your relationships will not be linear. Your future will not be linear. So stop expecting it to show up for you like that.

The steps you take won't always be forward. They won't always be right. And they won't always work out. But each *will* be the step that leads to another step that no matter where you go will be where you were meant to end up. For the lesson, for your own success, for the people, for you to heal, for you to grow, and for you to find your own, beautiful way.

Keep expecting curve balls and side steps. Know that you have everything within you to deal with them. And trust that it will all make sense in hindsight. The dots will connect. They always do. And when you look back, you will see for yourself that they always have.

Most likely, there's not going to be a time when you look around and decide that where you're at is the end-all, be-all of where you ever want to be. We are here to expand, just as the universe is ever expanding. Nothing will stay the same even when you're feeling confidently on your way. Because your arrival is now. Right now. And these actions you're taking now are enough to inspire you to keep pushing, and to inspire someone else to start.

REMEMBER WHAT YOU'RE A PART OF

You are the center of your own universe. It's true. Everything you see and experience and feel is from one perspective: your own. But this constant obsession over our own lives is often what keeps us at the edge of the game, on the sidelines, without ever actually jumping in. All you have to do is look out, from your own two eyes, and really see . . . really feel . . . really be. . . . There you'll find that rather than being alone, you're a part of a much bigger community that needs you, and a human experience that will humble you.

Don't just step, actually. You gotta jump in. Your path doesn't get discovered in your head. You can't think your way there. You can't think your way to confidence. You can't think your destination found. But you can get into your own life, and try to experience as much as possible with as many people as possible and remember that it's not all about you.

You're going to have a lot of ups and downs. When we're actually all in on trying things and picking up momentum, the natural fallout from that is real bumps—true bumps—on the path. And when those happen, and anytime you feel so absorbed in your head and your life and your unknowing and your problems, look up.

You're a part of something. Of a community, of a friend group, of a family, of a country, of a world that desperately needs us, right now, to believe that we can—and then go do whatever that *I can* feeling leads us to. Because in that doing is where we all create a world we want to be living in. It's where solutions are made, it's where stories are told, it's where paradigms shift, where boundaries are broken down, where norms are bucked, where shifts happen and changes are ushered in. That's you. That's not anyone else but you—all the yous of this thing and life that we're a part of.

And it'll help you remember what we established very early on: You're not alone in finding your way. You never have been.

DON'T DROP THE MIC; TURN IT UP

The first time I got profiled by a news outlet, it was none other than the first outlet I ever wrote for, the one that gave me my first column, the place I saw my first byline. It was, of course, my college newspaper. I remember thinking just how lovely and full circle it was to be written about in the place that I had spent years writing for.

I felt so giddy and grateful to be recognized for the work that set my soul on fire, and the not-so-traditional path I'd taken to get there. You can imagine what a buzzkill it was when a Facebook message popped up from someone telling me I'd gotten too big for my britches.

Ugh. I called my mom and cried for a hot second. Then I bitched to my roommates at the time. Each of them reminded me that the message I was sent wasn't true—I fit in my britches just fine. In hindsight I was facing what we all face when we begin to expand: the natural reaction some will have when we begin taking up space—with our clarity, with our confidence, with our expression, with our actions. It's the fallout of getting on your path, finding a little validation, and staying there.

You can imagine that years later as I sat with my best friends over champagne and doughnuts, watching my first appearance on *Good Morning America*, I had a flashback to that Facebook message and was like, *How about these big britches now, huh?*

Getting on the right path for yourself may mean getting off the path that others think is right for you. But here's what I want you to do with the successes you'll be finding, big and small, on the path of figuring this all out. I don't want you to drop the mic in dramatic glory. No, I want you to motion to the sound person in the back, and I want you to make sure the volume is all the way up. Work your ass off, and then allow yourself to be heard. Allow yourself to keep expanding and looking for bigger and clearer ways to get your work, your insights, your story, your energy out there. Whatever you do, don't stop working hard, because eventually your time will come. And when it does and you have the mic in your hand, keep it. That's when you can easily and swiftly pull other women into the light with you, and hand them the mic to amplify your work together.

But you can't wait for anyone other than *you* to turn that volume up.

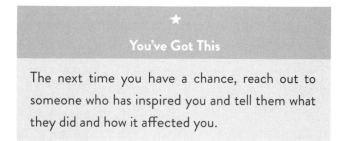

★

You've Got This

The next time you have a chance, reach out to someone who has inspired you and tell them what they did and how it affected you.

Big britches, contrary to nineties Victoria's Secret model sizes, are a goddamn glorious thing. You can and should talk about yourself like you actually dig this human you spend all your time with. Don't dim your own shine. For the love of lost, use your voice, your actions, your words, your stories to show the world what it means to actually believe in yourself and live a life according to *you*.

When you believe in yourself, your cup is full. It's what allows you to give back, to help, and to pull up the people and communities around you that need it. It's not egomania; it's fullness that runs over to benefit all the lives you're a part of.

You're here, so let's hear you fucking roar.

Here's what's super important about that roar. It's important that you get honest, really honest with what it took to get to your successes (even the mini ones). It doesn't mean being all down on yourself. It simply means letting people see beyond the highlight reel. You know when you're at a conference and the panel in front of you spends the hour telling their sweet stories of success? Well, I want you to be the one talking about your success *and* the shit days you had when nothing went right.

It shows we're human. It gives others watching your story some space to breathe, to know they can be confident in their abilities and still have a weird morning or year. It'll show them that they too can find direction without every day having to be perfect. Be a creator of moments that help others know they're not alone.

You can be open about your challenges and still be sure of yourself. You can detail the crap moments and still know and believe in your ability to get through it. You can have direction without knowing where it all ends up. Your story, your honest one, will fuel others to realize the same.

I'll leave you with this eloquent, well-thought-out, rewritten-about-seven-million-times final sentence, because they wouldn't let me put an f-word in the title (and because my mother would have killed me):

You're not fucking lost. You've got you. Show that you believe in yourself by taking the steps you dared to dream, and you'll have all the direction you've ever needed.

Arrived. Fully and wildly, you've arrived.

#batshitgrateful

There's not a font big enough for the title of this section. Or a hug long enough to appropriately express my appreciation. I owe the humans who helped bring this dream to life my heart.

My girlfriends—you know who you are. Near and far, the daily and the yearly. I'm a stronger, more confident, more loved, more all that is good and hopeful and divinely woman because of you. This book couldn't have been written without your friendship on the rough days, the lost days, the unsure days, and the exciting days. You're my greatest mirrors, my biggest inspirations, and my constant reminder of hope that we will rise.

The book dream team—Brandi for seeing and championing my vision every step of the way. Stephanie for beginning this process, Amanda for bringing it to life, and Lauren for seeing me through to the finish line.

The Real McCoys. You're my heart and soul. Thank you for giving me the foundation to keep building upon.

Tiffany Dufu, you opened this door. And you have been the greatest cheerleader, mentor, and fairy godmother as I ran my way through.

Carly Heitlinger, this book all started with #maxiemondays. Thank you for all of it. And for you.

Ellen McKay Lorenzo, thanks for picking up the phone call I'll never forget, and for the thousands after that I already have.

Kathleen Harris for bringing this title concept out of me at that conference table in 1 Union Square West. And all the work you did with my early proposal. Saint.

Healer Jim, for reminding me that I'm a princess warrior.

The Contro women, for your gorgeous book-writing haven.

The greatest impromptu whiteboard session that sealed the deal. Stine, I'm looking at you.

Caroline Eye for your quick read and brilliant insights.

The collective biz dream makers: Jessica Wuensch, for your sweet notes, your incredible talents, and your bright smile. Erica for always keeping my writing coherent and better than it began. Sarah Deragon for bringing out the best in me on camera. Erin and Luca, your design vision has carried me. Ansley, you keep all the online going.

Levo, my rocket ship. Every human on that team elevated my path in some way. And it all began with two. Amanda and Caroline, a forever thank-you.

Ronnie Martin, bringing me into your "Dream Job" vision made this book dream job possible.

My #diaryofabookdream supporters. Thank you for following along and sending me your support when I needed it most.

Piera, Carly, Latham, Jaclyn, Kristen, Ashley, Naomi, Tiffany, Marah, your interviews were gold. Your lives are remarkable. It's an honor to share your story and be a witness to your goodness. Thank you for being a part of this.

And to the thousands of women who led me here, those who welcomed me into their inbox, who signed up for my mentor circles, who showed up to my workshops, who read my words and shared them: Your stories and support have been my greatest gift. Without each of you and those uncountable conversations, this book would never have come to be. Thank you to the moon and back.

References

PRIMER

1   Oliver C. Robinson, Gordon R. T. Wright, and Jonathan A. Smith, "The Holistic Phase Model of Early Adult Crisis," *Journal of Adult Development* 20, no. 1 (2013): 27–37, http://eprints.bbk.ac.uk/6706/2/6706.pdf.

2   "Positive Neuroscience: 3 Ways to Wire Your Brain," Positive Psychology Program, September 7, 2015, https://positivepsychologyprogram.com/positive-neuroscience/.

3   "Confidence is the stuff that turns thoughts into action," quote from Dr. Richard Petty, The Ohio State University, in Katty Kay and Claire Shipman, *The Confidence Code* (New York: HarperCollins, 2014), chapter 2.

4   "What Is Newton's Third Law?" Khan Academy, https://www.khanacademy.org/science/physics/forces-newtons-laws/newtons-laws-of-motion/a/what-is-newtons-third-law.

CHAPTER 1

1   According to Allan G. Johnson's *The Gender Knot: Unraveling Our Patriarchal Legacy* (Philadelphia: Temple University Press, 2014), a society is patriarchal "to the degree that it is male-dominated, male-identified, and male-centered."

2   Drew Serres, "Why Patriarchy Persists (and How We Can Change It),"
     Organizing Change, https://organizingchange.org/patriarchy-persists-can
     -change/.
3   "Create & Cultivate NYC Keynote: Gloria Steinem," Vimeo video, 42:35,
     posted by Create & Cultivate, May 22, 2017, https://vimeo.com/218527013.
4   Vivian Hunt, Dennis Layton, and Sara Prince, "Why Diversity Matters,"
     McKinsey & Company, January 2015, http://www.mckinsey.com/business
     -functions/organization/our-insights/why-diversity-matters.
5   Technische Universität Darmstadt. "Facebook Makes Users Feel Envious,
     Dissatisfied: German Study Reveals Social Network's Big Role in Users'
     Emotional Life," ScienceDaily, January 21, 2013, www.sciencedaily.com
     /releases/2013/01/130121083028.htm.

CHAPTER 2

1   Alice Park, "Here's How to Make Waiting a Little Less Excruciating," *Time*,
     December 5, 2014, http://time.com/3619146/wait-more-patiently/.

CHAPTER 3

1   Kathy Caprino, "How Happiness Directly Impacts Your Success," *Forbes*, June
     6, 2013, https://www.forbes.com/forbes/welcome/?toURL=https://www.forbes
     .com/sites/kathycaprino/2013/06/06/how-happiness-directly-impacts-your
     -success/&refURL=https://www.google.com/&referrer=https://www.google
     .com/.

CHAPTER 4

1   Carol Dweck, "The Power of Believing That You Can Improve," filmed November
     2014 in Norrköping, Sweden, TED video, 10:21, https://www.ted.com/talks
     /carol_dweck_the_power_of_believing_that_you_can_improve?language=en.
2   George Loewenstein, "The Psychology of Curiosity: A Review and Reinter-
     pretation," *Psychological Bulletin* 116, no. 1 (1994): 75–98, http://www
     .cmu.edu/dietrich/sds/docs/loewenstein/PsychofCuriosity.pdf.
3   "Self-Confidence and Performance," in *Learning, Remembering, Believing:
     Enhancing Human Performance*, National Research Council (Washington, DC:
     National Academies Press, 1994), 173–206.

CHAPTER 6

1   Sally Andrews, David A. Ellis, Heather Shaw, and Lukasz Piwek, "Beyond Self-Report: Tools to Compare Estimated and Real-World Smartphone Use," *PLoS One* 10, no. 10 (2015): e0139004, http://journals.plos.org/plosone/article? id=10.1371/journal.pone.0139004.

2   Lysann Damisch, Barbara Stoberock, and Thomas Mussweiler, "Keep Your Fingers Crossed! How Superstition Improves Performance," *Psychological Science* 21, no. 7 (2010): 1014–20, http://journals.sagepub.com/doi/abs/10.1177 /0956797610372631.

3   Francesca Gino and Michael I. Norton, "Why Rituals Work," *Scientific American*, May 14, 2013, https://www.scientificamerican.com/article/why -rituals-work/.

4   Heather Barry Kappes and Gabriele Oettingen, "Positive Fantasies About Idealized Futures Sap Energy," *Journal of Experimental Social Psychology* 47, no. 4 (2011): 719–29, http://www.sciencedirect.com/science/article/pii/ S002210311100031X.

5   Charles Duhigg, *The Power of Habit: Why We Do What We Do in Life and Business* (New York: Random House, 2012).

6   Christian Jarrett, "How Expressing Gratitude Might Change Your Brain," *The Cut* (blog), *New York*, January 7, 2016, http://nymag.com/scienceofus/2016/01 /how-expressing-gratitude-change-your-brain.html.

CHAPTER 7

1   Margie Warrell, "Afraid of Being 'Found Out'? How to Overcome Impostor Syndrome," *Forbes*, April 3, 2014, https://www.forbes.com/sites/margiewarrell /2014/04/03/impostor-syndrome/#1004240248a9.

2   Julie Ma, "25 Famous Women on Impostor Syndrome and Self-Doubt," *The Cut* (blog), *New York*, January 12, 2017, https://www.thecut.com/2017/01 /25-famous-women-on-impostor-syndrome-and-self-doubt.html.

3   Richard Wiseman, "Self Help: Forget Positive Thinking, Try Positive Action," *Guardian*, June 30, 2012, https://www.theguardian.com/science/2012/jun/30 /self-help-positive-thinking.

CHAPTER 8

1   G. Richard Shell, *Springboard: Launching Your Personal Search for Success* (New York: Portfolio/Penguin, 2013).

2   Jeff Wise, "To Change Your Life, Learn How to Trust Your Future Self," *The Cut* (blog), *New York*, January 3, 2017, http://nymag.com/scienceofus/2017/01 /to-change-your-life-learn-how-to-trust-your-future-self.html.

CHAPTER 9

1   Bill von Achen, "'I'm Building a Cathedral!'—The Role of Purpose in Motivation," Best Practices for Business, May 7, 2010, https://bestpracticesforbusiness. com/2010/05/07/purpose-in-motivation/.
2   David Stoop, *You Are What You Think* (Grand Rapids, MI: Fleming H. Revell, 2003).
3   Christine Comaford, "Got Inner Peace? 5 Ways to Get It NOW," *Forbes*, April 4, 2012, https://www.forbes.com/sites/christinecomaford/2012/04/04/got-inner-peace-5-ways-to-get-it-now/#39783fbb6672.
4   Nichole Force, "Humor, Neuroplasticity and the Power to Change Your Mind," *World of Psychology* (blog), PsychCentral, https://psychcentral.com/blog/archives /2010/10/20/humor-neuroplasticity-and-the-power-to-change-your-mind/.
5   "What Is Brain Plasticity?" Your Brain Training, http://yourbraintraining.com /brain-plasticity.html.
6   Ohio State University, "Get Up on the Wrong Side of the Bed? Your Work Will Show It," EurekAlert! April 4, 2011, https://www.eurekalert.org/pub_releases /2011-04/osu-guo040411.php.
7   Adam Hadhazy, "Think Twice: How the Gut's 'Second Brain' Influences Mood and Well-being," *Scientific American*, February 12, 2010, https://www.scientific american.com/article/gut-second-brain/; Michael Mosley, "The Second Brain in Our Stomachs," *BBC News*, July 11, 2012, http://www.bbc.com/news /health-18779997.
8   Gordon Flett, Kirk Blankstein, Paul Hewitt, and Spomenka Koledin, "Components of Perfectionism and Procrastination in College Students," *Social Behavior and Personality: An International Journal* 20.2 (1992), http://www.yorku .ca/khoffman/Psyc3010/Flett'92_PerfProcr.pdf.
9   Eric Barker, "New Neuroscience Reveals 4 Rituals That Will Make You Happy," Ladders, May 19, 2017, https://www.theladders.com/p/21219/neuroscience-4 -rituals-happy.

CHAPTER 10

1   Bruna Martinuzzi, "The 90-Second Pause," American Express Open Forum, October 27, 2010, https://www.americanexpress.com/us/small-business /openforum/articles/the-90-second-pause-1/.

★ Notes ★

 Notes

★ Notes ★

★ Notes ★

★ Notes ★

★ Notes ★

Notes

★ Notes ★

 **Notes**

★ Notes ★

★ Notes ★

★ Notes ★

About the Author

Maxie McCoy is a writer and speaker obsessed with giving women the tools they need to believe in themselves. Committed to the global rise of women, she writes weekly inspiration and monthly curriculum on maxiemccoy.com. She is the host and executive producer of *Let Her Speak*, a live-audience show designed to lionize women's voices.

Maxie specializes in creating meaningful offline experiences that provide practical action in workshop and group formats. She's worked with top brands, conferences, and companies to create original events that engage their target audiences both online and off. Her work has been featured on *Good Morning America*, theSkimm, *Forbes*, *Fortune*, *INC*, *Bustle*, MyDomaine, *Women's Health*, *Marie Claire*, *Billboard*, CNN, and many more as an expert in women's leadership. Previously, Maxie built the Local Levo communities for Levo, a career platform for millennial women. During that time she scaled the ambassador program to thirty cities, launched their offline communities globally, and produced more than five hundred events with forty volunteer ambassadors. When she's not crafting sentences or rocking stages at conferences and corporate seminars, Maxie can be found surfing her favorite wave in Bali or painting with some shade of gold.